TEATROPHY
THREE MORE PLAYS

by

PETER CARLAFTES

THREE ROOMS PRESS

NEW YORK CITY

ISBN: 978-1-941110-13-3
Library of Congress Control Number: 2014916456

COVER AND BOOK DESIGN:
KG Design International
www.katgeorges.com

PUBLISHED BY:
Three Rooms Press, New York, NY
www.threeroomspress.com

DISTRIBUTED BY:
PGW/Perseus
www.pgw.com

*Shout out to Dave Zouzounis who
helped us carry this crazy dream*

TEATROPHY *(tē -atrəfē) "Teatro" is all things theater in Italian/Spanish derived
from the Latin theātrum. "Atrophy" is the gradual decline in effectiveness due to
underuse or neglect which derives from the Greek atrophia meaning "lack of food."
These three plays are food for all things theater. Take them and gorge yourself.
Then put more plays in the world. —PC*

On the cover: OUI, SORTIE *(acrylic on 5" × 7" canvas), painted by the author.
NOTE: When Marilyn Monroe Memorial Theater closed in August 2000, I decided to
paint a stage so Kat would always have a theater. The set is somewhat a hybrid
O'Neill's* The Iceman Cometh *and Pinter's* The Homecoming. *—PC*

INTRODUCTION

THERE I WAS: MID-THIRTIES, doing little to inspire much confidence in anyone, including myself, lost in the grind of trying to beat the grind with nothing more than a dream. Until I started performing my work in the Spoken Word scene. Something clicked. The pieces kept pouring out of me, so I read them each week at open mics. There was no pay. The reward was finding my voice.

Through the scene, I also found Kat Georges. Something else clicked. We began creating together. Ideas were our realm.

(or)

ONCE UPON A TIME I found myself living in a storefront theater space in South of Market San Francisco.

The year was 1993. The space Kat had started was Marilyn Monroe Memorial Theater at 96 Lafayette Street, a little alley off Mission near South Van Ness. About nine hundred square feet and fifty seats. There wasn't a kitchen. The stage was our stove.

The first play we did was Kat's *SCUM: The Valerie Solanas Story*, about the woman who shot Andy Warhol and invented her dream, the Society for Cutting Up Men. We found this incredible fluorescent ink, painted the set, and when the black light came up at the end of the play to change the entire set we were off to Never Never Land. Honing our craft.

Headshots came through the mail in droves. A dream inside every envelope.

Well, during the rehearsal phase of a play Kat and I co-wrote, *Wannabe*, we decided to paint the stage like a checkerboard, so we taped down many of those headshots to achieve the desired effect. Thus, quite a few actors were able to grace our stage and not even know.

We worked hard and long with a lot of great talent. We had a terrific company whose ethic was similar to ours: Create. If someone really needed the outside world, they were told that there was plenty of it out there, but inside the theater, we were perfecting another world with the sole intention to enlighten audiences.

Eight years and twenty-six original plays later—maybe no other two people on earth wrote, produced, and directed twenty-six original plays during that time—but this book isn't really a testament to that amazing accomplishment. Doing it is what turned us on. This book is a testament to the continual evolution of Theater despite its long-term decline as society's medium of choice.

TEATROPHY

Right here—these three plays are the thing.

—*Peter Carlaftes*

CONTENTS

TEATROPHY

If tomorrow comes, they'll kick its ass.

ANTI

an original play by
Peter Carlaftes

PRODUCTION NOTES:

The idea for *ANTI* came from a note I'd written years earlier in a compendium of true crime next to an entry for abolitionist riots in NYC (circa 1834) wherein those who were pro-slavery began burning down the houses of those who were not. In one instance, as a mansion burned, the crowd noticed that a large portrait of George Washington was about to be engulfed by flames; so they started shouting, "Don't burn the leader! Don't burn the leader!" and three people from the crowd dashed in, got the painting, then sat on the street, surrounding and protecting it. During another riot three days later, the angry mobs let it be known that any house that didn't have a candle burning in the window that night would be burned to the ground. And the note I wrote next to the entry in the book of crime was, "What will there be in the future to protect?" This became the basis of the play.

With inspiration from Beckett, Havel, and Pinter, I created three characters: Ave, Riddle, and Pierce. After deciding to play Pierce myself, I cast the roles Ave and Riddle before I wrote the play. Then with my two cast members (Ave sat on my left, SR, and Riddle on my right, SL), we sat on the stage facing the back wall and I typed the play out while talking through its inception with the cast, thinking that with this methodry, they would have all the motivation inherently instilled from being part of the creation. These are the types of places and angles you can find when it isn't only your pride and checkbook at stake. The play was written. Eighteen dense pages that never ended onstage in less than forty-five minutes—more often closer to an hour. The play is about creating density. The bleakness of the external you imagine assuages the emptiness inside.

ANTI is, above all, a perfect place to exist. Here it is now to be explored in this volume forever.

—*P. C.*

ANTI

SET:

The set is the stage of a theater. The audience perspective is from behind the stage, the opposite of their actual perspective. An empty, once elegant, simple four-legged wooden chair is positioned slightly CSR *facing* USL*. A mock candle with a switch-on video flame is positioned in a holder attached to the chair. A full length stage curtain, which opens by switch, covers three-fourths of the back wall starting* USR*. Where curtain ends (*USL*) there's a short wall containing switch for curtain, metallic holder, and futuristic phone.* DSR *is two-thirds straight wall back which has a 3 x 4 foot window centered in the second third, at which point a short wall angles* USL *that allows entry from behind. Two old, connected theater seats face* DSR *against short, angled wall. Outside window are pipes, tubes—dripping, rusting, pulsing. The window sill has a centered built-in holder. At* DSR *corner of the stage stands the dimensional façade of a large human skull. Rows of empty seats are painted on a backdrop behind* US *curtain.*

SERVANTS:

AVE: *unfulfilled dreamer*

RIDDLE: *subsidized rebel*

PIERCE: *government stooge*

START:

The time is a future day at early autumn dusk.

Music plays. Unreal light filters through window SL.
Music rises as light fades slowly.

Light off.

Music segues into sounds of infestation.
Sharp spotlight quickly shoots through window across stage.

SEQUENCE:

VOICE: *(Recording.)* Put a candle in the window.

AVE *enters in the dark and sits in chair,* CSR.

Sharp spotlight shoots through window again exposing AVE *to audience. Infestation sound begins to fade.*

Dark purple light rises slowly above AVE.

Short pause.

VOICE: *(Recording.)* Put a candle in the window.

RIDDLE *climbs in hurredly through window as if danger looms, backs up centered against* DSL *wall, and stretches both arms straight out against wall.*

Red light rises slowly on RIDDLE.

Long pause.

Infestation sound fades out.

AVE *stands in time, and crosses* SL *out window—short pause— then steps back and turns, facing* RIDDLE.

RIDDLE: *(Can't remember first line—*AVE*'s name. Fumbles.)* Ahhhhh . . .

AVE: *(Sharply.)* Ave.

RIDDLE: Of course! How could I forget such an original name? . . . Ave!

(Starts to go climb out window.)

AVE: Stop.

RIDDLE: What?

AVE: Stay.

RIDDLE: Where?

AVE: *(Motions to* RIDDLE'*s place against wall.)* There.

RIDDLE: *(Moves back to same position.)* Here?

AVE: Right where you are. *(Crosses* CS.*)* I see no need to start again.

RIDDLE: Ave.

AVE: *(Takes two steps back then turns to face* RIDDLE. *Pause.)* Do you have a candle?

RIDDLE: *(Checks pockets.)* Uh . . . no, I don't . . .

AVE: Pity. *(Crosses to chair and removes fake candle.)*

RIDDLE: But . . . I have a carrot! *(Reaches in back pocket, takes out carrot and holds out to* AVE.*)*

AVE: So I see.

AVE *crosses* SR *with candle, placing it in holder on windowsill.*

RIDDLE: I picked up a box at the Ponics on the way and stashed them just outside the window. . . .

AVE: *(Switches candle on; turns to* RIDDLE.*)* How resourceful. *(Crosses and sits motionless in chair.)*

RIDDLE *moves away from wall and looks at candle, then at* AVE. RIDDLE *crosses and slowly circles* AVE *counterclockwise.*

AVE: *(After* RIDDLE *makes one round.)* No.

RIDDLE: No? What? . . . You're not an illusion, too?

AVE: People don't talk like this.

RIDDLE: *(Crosses to the window and then sits on arm of* DS *theater chair.)* People used to watch you stare out the window . . . day after day after day . . . until you found the pain inside to be your only friend and no one had you ever since.

RIDDLE *slumps to the floor* CS.

RIDDLE: I wonder if I got the part. . . . Sometimes people are hard to read.

AVE: A child's face is hardest to draw . . . youth is flawless. . . .

PIERCE *enters and places metal folder dramatically in holder on wall by entryway.*

PIERCE: *(To* RIDDLE.*)* Are you?

RIDDLE: I don't know . . .

AVE: *(To both.)* Are . . . we . . . ?

PIERCE *admires the fake candle.* AVE *rises and picks up the skull on the prop cabinet.* RIDDLE *crosses to* PIERCE.

AVE: *(Picks up skull.)* Alas . . .

PIERCE: *(To candle.)* I like this. . . .

RIDDLE: *(To* PIERCE.*)* What's your purpose?

AVE: The picture has but seven plots.

PIERCE: My name's Pierce.

RIDDLE: Riddle over here.

AVE: This is a future where victims are the weapon.

PIERCE: I work for Subsidy.

RIDDLE: And I am a rebel.

AVE: *(Crosses and sits on* SR *theater seat.)* This is a theater . . . and we are the instruments of torture.

PIERCE: *(Picks up the skull.)* War! *(Dances a jig, moving skull's jaw.)* War!

RIDDLE *applauds wildly.*

AVE: *(To* RIDDLE.*)* I see the lonely critic in your heart of hearts.

RIDDLE: Ha! Think what you will . . . but I'm rebel to the bone . . . and, oh by the way . . . where have you been? . . . The critics got washed out years ago.

PIERCE: I cast my vote against their subsidy from the start. They had full status way past their purpose . . .

RIDDLE: Good riddance to those who don't think big.

PIERCE: (To AVE.) Hey . . . you want a carrot? . . . There's a box outside. . . . Glad to be of service, if you like. . . .

AVE *shoots* RIDDLE *a look of mistrust.*

PIERCE: *(Approaches* RIDDLE.*)* Hey . . . you want recognition? . . . Come with me. . . . I'll pull a few strings, if you like. . . .

RIDDLE *crosses* SL, *takes the carrot out and bites it.* AVE *sits in chair.*

AVE: Ave.

PIERCE: *(Hovering above* AVE.*)* Ave . . . what are your plans?

RIDDLE: *(Crosses to* SL *of* AVE.*)* Careful . . . you might fail to disappoint the audience.

PIERCE: *(Peeking behind curtain.)* There's no one there. . . .

AVE: *(Rises and crosses* SL.*)* Maybe that's what happened to God.

Noise-wave hits the room. AVE *and* RIDDLE *freeze.*

PIERCE: *(Looks at* AVE *and* RIDDLE *in amazement.)* Wow! *(Pulls the absorbeters out of his ear canals.)* These absorbeters really do the trick. *(Walks around between* AVE *and* RIDDLE *to make sure they are not aware.)* Hmmm . . . now, if I were to block this scene on a stage . . . I would put this one . . . over there . . . and this one . . . *(Belt lights up.)* Oh . . . *(Goes to phone gadget on the wall.)* Yes, Comrade . . . Pierce 409 reporting. . . . Theater 2, West Quadrant. . . . No, it's safe. . . . Yes. . . . No activity present. . . . One For All. . . . *(Returns attention to the frozen* AVE *and then* RIDDLE.*)* So . . . how do you like things down at the rebel dorm? . . .

Noise-wave hits and AVE *and* RIDDLE *become unstuck.* AVE *sits in her chair.* PIERCE *watches them to make sure they don't remember what happened.*

RIDDLE: *(Crosses to window.)* I forget what it is I'm supposed to grow out of. . . .

PIERCE: So . . . how do you like things down at the rebel dorm?

RIDDLE: Sorry, but . . . this seat is taken.

AVE: *(Turns her head to* RIDDLE *and* PIERCE *who sit next to each other on the theater seats.)* What do you want?

PIERCE: *(Rises.)* For years you dreamed you were a hero, and condoned a thousand petty lapses.

RIDDLE: Existentialism 101?

AVE: We're not in hell. . . .

PIERCE: And last year I played all three ghosts in the Subsidy production of *A Christmas Carol.*

RIDDLE: Next!

AVE: *(Stands and pulls the side curtain closed.)* The first impulse in life is . . . look at me. . . .

RIDDLE: Look what you've done.

AVE: *(Sits.)* And, who . . . by chance . . . will be left to create . . . without reward . . .

RIDDLE: *(Crosses to* AVE.*)* I don't get along well with the other rebels. They're jealous of me because my anger is rooted more deeply than their anger. . . . Just watch your monitor the next time they call in my squad to stage a riot and you'll see that I'm the one leading the pack. . . . (RIDDLE *pulls the side curtain back.)* The rest just go through the motions.

PIERCE: Hey . . . I'm a Culture Rep and I get around . . . but . . . well . . . you see . . . the problem is . . . I don't know how not to play the game.

RIDDLE: No soul . . . no guts . . . no fire inside.

PIERCE: Sometimes I dream, you know . . . about back when . . .

RIDDLE: Oh no . . . I was born too late.

PIERCE: And what it must've felt like to be on the stage.

RIDDLE: *(Paces.)* What to do . . . what to do . . . keeps time a-wasting. . . .

PIERCE: I take a bow in my dream . . .

RIDDLE: What to do . . . what to do . . .

PIERCE: But . . .

RIDDLE: Unrest seeps through my pores.

PIERCE: Nothing comes back.

AVE: Welcome to a world of quiet desperation.

Pause.

PIERCE: How do you get to the place where you know that what you need is real?

RIDDLE: Let's see . . . you take a right at the corner . . .

RIDDLE *continues directions until the phone gadget rings.* AVE *answers.*

AVE: Theater 2. . . . No. . . . There will be no performance tonight.

AVE *crosses to prop table and fiddles around.* PIERCE *notices that she is barefoot and removes his shoes.*

AVE: Pierce . . . what is it you wish to propose?

PIERCE: Well . . . I think . . . the three of us . . . should . . . do a show here live . . . without the monitor. . . .

RIDDLE: *Marat Sade: The Musical.*

PIERCE: You should be seen but not heard.

RIDDLE: Watch it . . . I know sign language.

AVE: *(To both.)* Tell me where your needs fit into this. . . .

PIERCE: Uh . . .

RIDDLE: I think the spy who came in just got cold.

AVE: *(Sits.)* There will be no performance tonight.

A trumpet player practices scales somewhere nearby.

Pause.

RIDDLE *lays down flat stage right.* PIERCE *returns to the downstage theater seat.*

RIDDLE: They'll let you practice in this world for as long as you want.

AVE: Jazz is like a drunk who walks perfect.

PIERCE: I really . . . admire . . . jazz . . . the freedom . . . I have no outlet for. . . . The others . . . on my crew . . . I know . . . and the neighbors . . . none of them. . . .

RIDDLE: Never tell them where you're gonna land.

Pause.

PIERCE: *(To* AVE.*)* Do you know who's playing?

AVE: Yeah . . . it's me. . . . At least sometimes . . . I think it's me . . . between notes.

RIDDLE: A rebel ain't got time for nothing in between.

AVE *rises to prop cabinet and pulls up a dance bar and does stretching, then interpretive dance.* RIDDLE *pulls out a piece of chalk and begins to draw an outline on the stage around her body.* AVE *dances.* PIERCE *bites his toenails. The music comes in and out. Silence until the music ends.*

After the music stops, AVE *comes out of her spell and lowers the dance bar. The sound brings* RIDDLE *and* PIERCE *back.* RIDDLE *puts the chalk away, stands, and admires her outline.*

RIDDLE: *(Crosses to* AVE.*)* You want me to leave?

AVE: *(Looks at* PIERCE.*)* Not yet.

Pause. AVE *stands stage right of the side curtain.* RIDDLE *circles* AVE's *chair.*

PIERCE: *(Stands.)* How do you escape the fact that nothing is enough?

RIDDLE: Well . . . the line I hold is this: I don't give, I don't take . . . and I don't want nothing. . . .

AVE: Nothing is enough.

RIDDLE: I know if I find what I want . . . they'll take it . . . and if I slow down . . . they'll take me. . . . Roses might be blooming out there . . . but in here . . . in here's full of pus . . . and let me tell you something . . . it's gonna blow soon . . . and when it does . . . I'm gonna be there. (RIDDLE *slumps down in* AVE's *chair, catches her breath, then sits up straight.)*

AVE *sits on the arm of the downstage theater seat and stares out the window with growing contempt.* PIERCE *crosses and stands straight in front of the side curtain edge between* AVE *and* RIDDLE.

AVE: Alone, in silence . . . I lived my purpose once . . . because the pictures in my head weren't painted by me. . . .

RIDDLE: My agent said the Media will promote me to revolutionary status . . . just as soon as the right cause comes along. . . .

AVE *and* RIDDLE *stare at each other.*

PIERCE: I heard the monitor's fully automated now. . . . The cameras operate . . . on body heat . . . or something like that. . . .

AVE: *(Slowly falls apart.)* When I speak . . . the words sound as if they were . . . preapproved. . . . Like . . . OK . . . I can say . . . My name is Ave . . . I sit in a theater and watch my thoughts collect dust . . . but I'm safe . . . behind the curtain. . . . So . . . What's your purpose? . . . *(*RIDDLE *slides out of the chair and crawls across the floor to* AVE. PIERCE *looks down into the outline on his hands and knees.)* They provide me with certainty for life. . . . And all they ask in return is the candle in a window. . . . So . . . each night . . . I put one in my window . . . but the candle that I use isn't real . . . because they were wrong to take my tomorrows.

RIDDLE: *(At the same time.)* They were right about one thing, though . . . *(Stops.)*

PIERCE: They were right about one thing, though . . . There's no way to control the fine line between killing something and creating a masterpiece. . . .

Pause.

PIERCE: *(Sits up.)* What they figured out about us was so simple. . . . I mean . . . the crime rate's close to nil and suicide's practically non-existent. . . . Why . . . it's like . . .

RIDDLE: Heaven on earth . . .

AVE: Peace at last . . .

PIERCE: *(Stands up.)* Listen . . . I have a confession to make. . . .
Before the music . . . the both of you were frozen by . . .
A Centauri Interim. *(Dramatically awaits response but* AVE *and*
RIDDLE *are off in their own world.)* That's a new pulse wave
Technique designed so Subsidy can secretly contact their field
agents. . . . *(Pause. . . . No response.)* See this little gizmo? . . .
Absorbs the sound so I don't freeze, too.

AVE: They leave nothing to chance.

RIDDLE: Accidents do still happen, though.

PIERCE: I don't know why I'm telling you this . . . I could lose my
purpose. . . .

RIDDLE: Look . . . none but a few know just how many . . . poor
risks . . . remain . . . inside the boundaries of Reality.

PIERCE: My three weeks in Sanctuary comes up soon and the last
thing I need is Redirection.

RIDDLE: Those Clash Action Suits Abovesurface are pure fog. . . .
See, I'm not a rebel . . . I work Conflict under counter . . . and
believe me . . . the process of elimination isn't pretty. . . . The
world needs disorder and I'm the supplier. . . . So . . . when I get
called . . . a bomb goes off . . . at the right time . . . in the wrong
place. . . .

PIERCE: I hear Sanctuary has a hot new place called Crime Pays. . . .
You want to rob a bank? . . . You go in and rob a bank. . . .

RIDDLE: For instance . . . take today. . . . They sent me west with a
bomb inside a box of carrots. . . .

AVE: They pacify our deep-set sorrow with this dream come true. . . .

RIDDLE: The target for today . . .

AVE: If you wish to continue . . .

RIDDLE: The target for today, is . . .

AVE: Your dream come true . . .

RIDDLE: What's the target for today? . . .

AVE: Just tell them . . . No . . .

PIERCE: *(Whispers to* RIDDLE.*)* Theater 2 . . .

RIDDLE: The target for today is theater number two . . .

AVE: There will be no performance tonight.

PIERCE: *(To* RIDDLE.*)* And . . .

RIDDLE: And? . . .

AVE: If you wish to cancel . . .

RIDDLE: And when it blows . . .

AVE: Your dream come true . . . just tell them . . . Yes . . .

RIDDLE: I'm gonna be there . . .

AVE: I'm not complete . . . then . . . the dream terminates at that point. . . .

AVE *rises and begins to orchestrate the movements of* RIDDLE *and* PIERCE.

AVE: I'm ready.

PIERCE: *(To* RIDDLE.*)* Are you . . . ?

RIDDLE: *(To* PIERCE.*)* I don't know. . . .

RIDDLE and PIERCE: *(To* AVE.*)* Are we . . . ?

AVE: I'm in control.

PIERCE: Are you?

RIDDLE: I don't know.

PIERCE: *(Frightened.)* Am I?
and
RIDDLE: Are we?

AVE: The time turns now but once . . .

PIERCE: So true.

RIDDLE: So true.

AVE: Here comes my echo.

RIDDLE and PIERCE: The time turns now but once.

AVE: Which came first . . . the victim or the weapon?

PIERCE: *(Whispers to* RIDDLE.*)* The weapon.

RIDDLE: *(Answers* AVE.*)* The weapon. (AVE *shakes her head.)*

PIERCE: *(Shouts.)* The victim. *(Smiles.)*

RIDDLE: *(Too late.)* The victim. . . .

AVE: The one beat down where the other began. . . .

PIERCE: I think I can . . . I gave my all.

RIDDLE: I think I can . . . I gave my all.

AVE: The cut time cold lost step in the middle. . . . Solo. . . .

PIERCE: I've got a good life . . . with all the basics . . . and then some. . . . So it's clear why my needs . . . really don't . . .

RIDDLE: Now you tell me . . . what could be better? . . . I can't complain . . . and when I do . . . I get paid extra. . . .

AVE: *(Rising on chair.)* Homo . . . Stasis . . .

PIERCE: One for all. . . . One for all. . . .

RIDDLE: What's in it for me?

PIERCE: One for all. . . . One for all. . . .

RIDDLE: What's in it for me?

PIERCE: One for all. . . . One for all. . . .

RIDDLE: What's in it for me?

AVE: There's only one ultimate whole. . . .

PIERCE: One for all. . . . One for all. . . .

RIDDLE: What's in it for me?

PIERCE: One for all. . . . One for all. . . .

RIDDLE: What's in it for me?

PIERCE: One for all. . . . One for all. . . .

RIDDLE: What's in it for me?

AVE: Whether it be mind or matter . . .

PIERCE: Or some third thing . . .

RIDDLE: That's the basis of both.

Pause. AVE *crosses* DS *and pushes button opening back curtain revealing flat of empty, decrepit theater house.*

AVE: *(returning to chair—sinks slowly.)* For . . . one . . . I'm not . . . what's . . . in me. . . .

PIERCE *and* RIDDLE *snap out of the flow.* RIDDLE *returns to same wall as on entry.* PIERCE *takes the metal folder from the shelf and stands same place as entry.* AVE *hides behind her chair. Pause.*

AVE: *(Rising to her knees by chair facing out.)* I remember a story . . . that I read once in Revival . . . from *The Book of Anger* . . . About a group . . . long ago . . . who didn't want the world to change. . . . Not that they were happy with the world . . . you see. . . . only . . . driven by the need to be heard. . . . But the world wouldn't listen . . . so . . . they set fire to their city. . . . And somewhere . . . above the flames . . . hung the portrait of a leader. . . . A lone voice cried out, "Don't burn the leader!" . . . And soon . . . the whole crowd . . . was chanting along . . . "Don't burn the leader!" . . . Then, three came forth . . . and took the painting . . . away from the fire. . . . Now . . . the story didn't say . . . who these three were . . . or why. . . . *(Stands next to chair and a very strong pull between the three takes place.)* But . . . there . . . they found the need to preserve . . . an illusion . . . and . . . together . . . by chance . . . in the midst of all this madness . . . *(Sits.)* They . . . had a purpose. . . .

Pause. PIERCE *hands metal folder to* AVE. *He turns to leave and notices his feet are bare. He smiles and turns to* AVE, *but she is looking at* RIDDLE. PIERCE *pushes button which begins back curtain closing and exits.* AVE *notices that* PIERCE *is gone.* AVE *looks once more at* RIDDLE *then opens the folder.* RIDDLE *climbs out the window and disappears.* AVE *looks back at closed curtain then the open folder.* RIDDLE *reaches in and swipes the candle.*

AVE: *(Reads from folder.)* The light fades . . . above Ave.

AVE *smiles and closes the folder as the light fades above* AVE.

Blackout.

Long pause.

Music begins. AVE *exits. Window light rises, same as before.*

THE . . . END . . .

CLOSURE.

A PSYCHO-SEXUAL THRILLER

welcome
to

the bitter end.

A PLAY BY
PETER CARLAFTES

PRODUCTION NOTES:

"Closure" was a word being bandied around in the mid-1990s like some kind of a be/end-all antitoxin. Poof. Say the word: "Closure." I began to write a play called *Closure* starting with this preface:

PREFACE:
Closure.
(Latin) claudere > to close
(Webster's) a closing; finish; an end

PRELUDE:
Today, as it stands, mythology's defunct. "God" became a word; likewise—
"Closure." Those glad it's not them, keep abreast of those that are (i.e. murder
victims' families, victims of monumental disasters) hoping for the best
(i.e. closure). In time, when right's left, and vice versa (more closure), the
dysfunctional will then deem those healthy pariahs.

Little by little, the four characters unfolded and later, in hindsight, I realize how much I owe Genet's *The Maids* and strangely enough Raymond Chandler's *The Big Sleep* as inspirations. Playing the main character Rig was such a blast after shaving off my eyebrows. No one in the theater would come near me. Kat was scared to death of me.

Best thing that could've happened. I knew we had a play. And when many people who saw it told me they didn't look at people the same way afterward, I knew it hit the mark.

Now it's here for you to explore.

—*P. C.*

CLOSURE.
A Play

Welcome
to

the
Bitter End

PREFACE:
Closure.
(Latin) claudere > to close
(Webster's) a closing; finish; an end

PRELUDE:
Today, as it stands, mythology's defunct. "God" became a word; likewise— "Closure." Those glad it's not them, keep abreast of those that are (i.e. murder victims' families, victims of monumental disasters) hoping for the best (i.e. closure). In time, when right's left, and vice versa (more closure), the dysfunctional will then deem those healthy pariahs.

CHARACTERS

MEA RANDOM: *Thirty-one, alone; can't face world; doesn't have to, rich; beach house, Santa Monica; hiding secrets, in therapy, abused by father; holding guilt, sister* PHELONE *killed father, mother killed self; ruled murder-suicide, she never told*

SIDNEY (DR. MERIT): *Forty, psychologist; lives/works: Venice; never married,* MEA's *doctor; kept numb by others' pain*

RIG MANTES: *Thirty-five, ex-con; three weeks on parole; prison case study, two years ago for* DR. MERIT; *active death wish, did time for rape*

PHELONE RANDOM: *Twenty-four, doll-like;* MEA's *younger sister; lives inside family house, near Burbank airport; self-absorbed, had parents stuffed*

ACT I.

SCENE 1

PART 1:
SIDNEY's *office;* SIDNEY *&* MEA;
Tuesday; Early Afternoon

PART 2:
MEA's *house;* MEA *&* RIG;
Tuesday; 9 p.m.

DARK
INTERLUDE:
MEA's *house;* MEA;
Dawn; Next Day

SCENE 2

PART 1:
SIDNEY's *office;* SIDNEY;
Morning; Five Hours Later

PART 2:
PHELONE's *house;* PHELONE;
Wednesday; Same Time

DARK
INTERLUDE:
Telephone conversation; PHELONE *&* RIG;
Early Afternoon; Five Days Later

SCENE 3

PART 1:
SIDNEY's *office;* SIDNEY *&* MEA;
Tuesday; Same Time

FLASHBACK:
Conversation; MEA *&* RIG;
Last Week

PART 2:
PHELONE's *house;* PHELONE *&* RIG;
Tuesday; Thirty Minutes Later

DARK
INTERLUDE:
Tape recording; SIDNEY *&* SONTAG;
Wednesday Afternoon

SCENE 4

PART 1:
MEA's *house;* MEA *&* TV;
Wednesday; Same Time

PART 2:
SIDNEY's *office;* SIDNEY *&* RIG;
Same Time

DARK

INTERMISSION

ACT I.

SCENE 1

PART 1:
SIDNEY's *office;*
Tuesday; Early Afternoon

SET:

DSL; *Desk, two chairs, painting, computer, video screen with X-ray image of moving reel to reel machine when turned on, bookshelf, books, degrees. Open doorway* USL, *revealing small anteroom and entrance.*

Office opens. SIDNEY *(behind desk)* & MEA *(other chair) in place.*

Music fades. MEA *begins.*

MEA: *(Drawn out.)* Uhhh . . . *(Light fades up.)* You're saying . . .

SIDNEY: *(Quickly.)* No, Mea. Merely suggesting . . .

MEA: That, I . . . get "involved?"

SIDNEY: Well?

MEA: Come on. With my baggage?

SIDNEY: Live in the present.

MEA: There's nothing "there."

Pause.

SIDNEY: Here.

MEA: Nothing's "here."

Pause.

SIDNEY: Silence.

MEA: Yeah . . .

SIDNEY: Then, that's "something."

MEA: It's, been too long . . . since I've been held . . .

SIDNEY: *(Quick.)* Do you want to be held?

MEA: I don't want to be held. *(Pause.)* I wouldn't be held like . . .
I want to be held . . .

SIDNEY: Then . . . you want to be held.

MEA: I don't need . . . to be held. *(Pause.)* I've got you.

SIDNEY: You're alone.

MEA: *(Quick.)* I see it . . .

SIDNEY: What?

MEA: The microphone—there. . . . *(Points to bookshelf.)* Second shelf . . .

SIDNEY *makes notation.*

MEA: It soothes me, Sidney, finding the microphone.

SIDNEY: A dose of cognizance.

MEA: Our little game . . .

Pause.

MEA: *(Drifting.)* You know, last week, I . . . noticed something funny,
a . . . small detail . . . about shampoo . . . *(Pause.)* I was taking a
shower . . . I reached for the bottle. . . . Now, when I wash my hair,
I use tons of shampoo . . . always have . . . don't know why . . .
I indulge myself, then. . . . *(Pause.)* So, I picked up the bottle. . . .
It's halfway full . . . I thought, "Wait . . . I bought this, what? . . .
Five weeks ago" . . . Started reading the label. . . . It was green, for
dry scalps . . . so, I guess . . . knowing that . . . you don't use quite
as much . . . *(Pause. Snaps back.)* I never bought . . . a shampoo . . .
with medicine before. . . .

Pause.

SIDNEY: Define . . . for me simply . . . now, what you feel?

MEA: *(Quick.)* Reverence.

SIDNEY: Reverence?

MEA: Reverence . . .

SIDNEY: Toward . . .

MEA: Well . . . you, for one . . .

SIDNEY: Why?

MEA: You understand.

SIDNEY: I'm paid . . .

MEA: You enjoy . . . what you do.

Pause.

SIDNEY: When's the last time you shared a laugh with a stranger? Ready or not . . . you deserve more.

MEA: Sidney, I'm convinced . . . "more" isn't enough . . . and besides . . . it's a four-letter word . . .

SIDNEY: *(Quick.)* So is "Hell."

MEA: How to serve penance, in . . . thirty years or less, ha. Oh, by the way . . . has, Phelone called?

SIDNEY: *(Flips notebook one page back.)* Not since . . . last session. Why? *(Pause.)* Something wrong?

MEA: Well, I hate that house, I mean . . . you know my sister. . . . How she can live there . . . is way beyond me. . . . But I love her . . . she's all . . . I feel love. So, I figure . . . the more she connects to . . . the outside world . . . that much better off . . . she will be. . . . *(Pause.)* Right?

SIDNEY: I suggest you consider . . . the same approach. . . . *(Pause.)* Get involved.

MEA *fidgets. Composes herself. Interlude begins with recording of her voice, repeating inside, "Get involved . . . Get involved," while light fades.* SIDNEY *exits.* MEA *disrobes. Sound continues.*

Set change.

PART 2:
MEA's house;
Tuesday; 9 p.m.

SET:
USL. *Couch, matching throw rug; cell phone, end table, TV monitor; window (over couch), curtain; blanket, magazines; photograph on wall in frame (two girls ages five or six and twelve or thirteen); exit out of view,* SL; *background sound of waves.*

MEA's *house opens.* MEA *and* RIG's *clothes, already in place.*

MEA *(In slip, on couch, supine) and nude* RIG *(on top of her).*

In the dark: Shorebreak background sound begins. Sounds of MEA *and* RIG, *making love, start to rise.* MEA's *"get involved" slowly fades.* MEA *and* RIG *climax. Light fades up.* RIG *slides off couch.*

RIG: *(Stretching legs out, leans back against couch; pulls up underwear.)* I'm an only child. . . .

MEA: Mmm . . .

RIG: You an only child?

MEA: No . . . I have a sister.

Pause.

RIG: Older?

MEA: Younger . . . *(Pause.)* Seven years younger . . .

RIG: And, you?

MEA: *(Frowns.)* Thirty-one . . .

RIG: *(Quick.)* What's her name?

MEA: Pardon?

RIG: Does your sister have a name . . .

MEA: Oh . . . Phelone . . . It's Phelone.

RIG: *(Laughs)* No shit! . . . Like the "Crime" . . .

MEA: No, P-H-E-, L-O-, N-E . . . Phelone. She's beautiful . . .

RIG: She live nearby?

MEA: *(Cold.)* Enough about my sister, Rig. . . . *(Softens.)* How old . . . are you?

RIG: Thirty-five . . . *(Pause.)* Beat Christ . . . by two years . . . *(Pause.)* What time you got?

MEA: *(Startled.)* Uhhh . . . just past seven. Why?

Pause.

RIG: Don't worry, Sugar . . . I'm staying the night.

MEA: Tell me something, Rig. . . . Is that your real name?

RIG: What do you think?

MEA: I don't know. . . . *(Pause.)* Sounds like a nickname . . .

RIG: It's "real."

MEA: I believe you . . .

RIG: Okay, how's this? . . . My given name was Rick. . . . Just Rick . . . Plain Rick . . . when I was little . . . Rick Mantes. So . . . they made fun of my name at school, you know. . . . "Look, there's Rick. Hey, Rick, you're a dick . . ." I tell you, it . . . got to me. . . . *(Pause.)* But there was this one kid, what the fuck was his name? . . . Had some disease. . . . He was all messed up. . . . *(Laughs.)* Head about the size of a grapefruit. . . . *(Pause.)* Anyhow, he . . . was hard to understand. . . . One day, he called me "RIGGG" . . . and I liked it. So . . . I told the other kids I . . . changed my name. . . . *(Pause.)* And none of them . . . mocked me . . . ever again. . . .

Pause.

MEA: Why is it . . . children are basically . . . cruel . . . ?

RIG: Uh-huh . . .

MEA: Makes no sense . . .

RIG: Makes perfect sense, Sugar . . .

MEA: Girls even more so . . . than boys. *(Pause.)* I don't . . . want . . . *(Pause.)* I can't . . . have . . .

Pause.

RIG: Mea, we got something in common . . .

Long pause.

RIG: You know, that tale . . . I told you before . . . the one about my name? . . . *(Pause.)* None of it was true. . . . But you sympathized, with me . . . heart and soul. . . . Because of the retard . . . you bought it.

Pause.

MEA: What else do . . . you do . . . besides lie . . . and fuck . . . ?

RIG I wait . . . only now . . . I know more. . . . Listen, Sugar. . . . *(Light begins to fade.)* After learning . . . how to talk . . . first . . . time I said . . . my name, "Rick" . . . it came, out . . . "Rig" and . . . my parents were . . . tickled. So . . .

MEA: Point well-hidden. *(Pause.)* You were right. We do have something . . . in common.

Light off. Shorebreak sound rises. RIG *exits.* MEA *sleeps on couch.*

DARK INTERLUDE:
MEA's *house;*
Dawn; Next Day

Shorebreak fades to same volume as Part 2. Dawn light (in window) rises. MEA *wakes up, looks around.* RIG's *gone.* MEA *sits up.*

MEA: I thought . . . men, didn't leave . . . *(Pause.)* How would I know . . . ?*(Picks up cell phone, presses button.)* Must tell . . . Sidney. . . . *(Listens; repeats* SIDNEY's *unheard message.)* This is the office of . . . Sidney Merit . . . *(Dawn light fades.)* Please wait . . . before starting your message . . . for the series of beeps . . . to end. . . .

Dawn light out. Shorebreak sound fades. MEA *exits. Playback of* MEA's *message (loud beep) begins.*

ACT I.

SCENE 2

PART 1:
SIDNEY's *office;*
Morning; Five Hours Later

*Set change (*MEA*'s house to* MERIT*'s office) during playback of* MEA*'s message.*
SIDNEY *(behind desk) in place.*

MEA'S MESSAGE: Well, it happened . . . Strange, Sidney. . . . By the way,
It's . . . Mea Random. . . . Early Wednesday morning . . . God, about
dawn. . . . *(Pause.)* What am I doing? . . . I'm . . . leaving you a
message. . . . *(Pause.)* I met a man yesterday . . . outside your office.
. . . We . . . came back to my place. . . . *(Pause.)* Now, he's gone. . . .
(Pause.) Thin air. . . . Is that what they're like . . . ? *(Pause. Light
rises on* SIDNEY *writing.)* I don't know, I don't think . . . I even liked
him. *(Pause.)* His name was . . . *(Noise.)* God, Rig! . . . He's . . .

RIG'S VOICE: *(On tape.)* Been here all the time. . . . *(Pause.)* Who's
Sidney?

MEA'S MESSAGE: A "friend." Uhhh, look, I . . . talk soon. . . . Bye. . . .
(Click.)

SIDNEY *looks concerned. The name "Rig" sounds familiar. Loud beep;*
PHELONE*'s message (with eerie doll-house music) begins.*

PHELONE'S MESSAGE: Doctor, doctor . . . it's me, Phelone . . . calling to
"wish" that . . . it was your birthday. . . . When is your birthday?
Mine's Feb fourteenth . . . uh-huh, Valentine's day . . . *(Pause.)* Is it
true? . . . Cupid never grew up? . . . If so, then . . . neither . . . will
I. . . . Me, my . . . Do you think there are . . . others . . . like "me?"
. . . Am I bad? . . . Do you think . . . are there "others" . . . like
"me?" . . . *(Pause. Same eerie dollhouse music rises from speaker in*
PHELONE*'s house* DR. MERIT*'s office light slowly fades.)* Let's see,
what else . . . ? *(Pause.)* How's Mea, my sister? . . . You saw her last
. . . *(Pause.)* I know . . . something . . . happened. . . .

Lights out. SIDNEY *exits. Eerie dollhouse music continues.*

SCENE 2

PART 2:

PHELONE's *house;*
Wednesday; Same Time

SET: USR; *dining room counter, two stools, breakfast nook; small table; kitchen entry* USR; *family room doorway,* USC, *(open) reveals two sets of chair legs and feet of stuffed parents, with enough room to enter past TV on rolling stand.*

Set change to PHELONE's *house.* PHELONE *(crouched under counter) in place. Light rises. Eerie dollhouse music fades.*

PHELONE: *(Pretending to be a little girl, playing "sex slave" with an imaginary friend.)* Mommy! . . . Oh, Mother, Ma! . . . I can't find Dad's handcuffs. What? . . . Yes, I looked in the drawer, Ma. . . . Yes, it's important . . . I'm playing with . . . what's your name? . . . Lizzie Borden, my . . . best, best friend . . . in the world, ain't 'cha Lizzie? . . . I can't ask her to leave, Ma! . . . That's not polite. . . . How 'bout "steak knives" instead? Ahh . . . you're no fun. . . . Get out! . . . She's gone . . . Ma . . . I did what you said. . . . *Climbs out from behind stools, stands, enters kitchen. Returns with steak knife, sits at table, carves name.)* Pain, pain . . . go away. . . . *(Scratches out name on table.)* Fuck up someone else's day . . . *(Rises.)* Pain, pain . . . *(Drops knife on table, returns to kitchen.)* Daddy's got . . . a "hard on." *(Enters dancing.)* Daddy's got . . . *(Sticks head in family room.)* . . . a "hard on." . . . Mom, whose . . . turn is it? . . . I did it . . . last time . . . London Bridge is . . . Daddy's got a "hard on." Again. Again . . . He didn't want, me. . . . Again and again and again. . . . Father, please . . . want "me," for once. . . . I got a knife. . . . Serve from the "left" . . . Bedroom? Or kitchen? . . . Slash—I'm confused. *(Sits at table.)* You know, there are days that I want a dick . . . you know. Want . . . a dick. . . . Not, "want" one . . . I'd like to . . . have one. . . . Just like Dad's. . . . *(Sings.)* Wouldn't that be nice? . . . *(Light begins to fade. Scratches table with knife.)* Wouldn't it? . . . Wouldn't it? . . . Wouldn't it? . . .

Light out. PHELONE *exits. Sound of waves rises.*

DARK
INTERLUDE:
Telephone conversation
Early Afternoon; Five Days Later

Set change: PHELONE's *house to* MERIT's *office. Recording of conversation begins.* RING . . . RING . . . RIG *answers . . . Silence.*

PHELONE: Mea? . . . Are you there?

RIG: Hello . . .

PHELONE: *(Aside.)* Oh, right. . . . She's with the doctor. . . . And, to "whom" . . . am I speaking? . . .

RIG: Rig.

PHELONE: What kind of name is that?

Pause.

RIG: What kind of name . . . is Phelone?

PHELONE: How'd you know my . . . who are you?

RIG: Your sister's . . . boyfriend . . .

PHELONE: Liar!

Pause.

RIG: Don't call me that.

PHELONE: You didn't say, "Please" . . . *(Pause.)* If I tell you where I live . . . will you come visit?

RIG: I'd like that.

PHELONE: When?

RIG: Real soon . . .

Shorebreak recording fades. SIDNEY *and* MEA *in place.*

SCENE 3

PART 1
SIDNEY's *office;*
Tuesday; Same Time

MEA: Sidney, I'm sorry. What was the question?

SIDNEY: Given the chance . . . would you tell "them" the truth?

Pause. Light rises.

MEA: I had to . . . protect her.

SIDNEY: Should we . . . change topics?

Pause.

SIDNEY: What about . . . the man you met . . . ?

MEA: *(Overlapping "you met.")* Rig.

SIDNEY: *(Hesitates; something clicks.)* What about "Rig?"

MEA: There's . . . not much, to tell. Thirty-five. Loner type. *(Pause.)* What can I say? He's still at . . . my house.

SIDNEY: You mean now?

MEA: *(Nods.)* Never left . . .

SIDNEY: Was this your decision?

MEA: He just . . . sort of happened . . . to move in . . . with me.

SIDNEY: Where'd he live before?

Pause.

MEA: In a station wagon.

SIDNEY: Rather "impulsive."

MEA: He's . . . down on his luck.

SIDNEY: And now you believe . . . you can change all that?

MEA: We're on . . . the same path.

SIDNEY: Alluding . . . to what?

MEA: You said, "Get a life," Sidney. Fate intervened.

SIDNEY: Not as much . . . as you've . . . counteracted.

Pause.

MEA: You mean it's "my" fault . . . the man said, "Hello."

SIDNEY: Mea. I'm a little . . . concerned.

Light begins to fade.

MEA: He never said, "Hello." He said, "Twins." . . . and pointed. Sitting on the hood of . . . his shitty, old car. At first, I thought he meant . . . did I . . . have a twin? But, when I looked . . . there, they were . . . in a two-seated stroller. A set of . . . twin boys . . . sleeping, side by side.

Light fades. Flashback begins. SIDNEY *&* MEA *exit.*

Set change: MERIT's *office to* PHELONE's *house.*

FLASHBACK:
Conversation:
Last Week

RIG: *(Mumbles.)* Letters . . .

MEA: What letters?

RIG: Our names . . . have three letters.

MEA: So . . .

RIG: "Little" things, on the whole, Sugar . . . make us alive. You know, things like . . . us both having, three-letter names.

MEA: Where you from?

Pause.

RIG: The north.

MEA: Pole?

RIG: Cute.

MEA: *(Laughs.)* You Arctic?

RIG: Look closer. I'm here, Mea. Nothing else . . . matters. Every place, I been . . . up till now . . . found you.

Pause.

MEA: I don't even . . . want me.

RIG: What you want . . . hasn't happened. *(Pause.)* But . . . it will.

MEA: When?

RIG: With me. In time.

Interlude ends. PHELONE *&* RIG *in place.*

SCENE 3:

PART 2
PHELONE's *house;*
Tuesday; Thirty Minutes Later

RIG *has just entered* PHELONE's *house.*

RIG: So, you're seven years younger?

PHELONE: Uh-huh.

Light rises.

RIG: Seven's a good number.

PHELONE: Is that supposed to . . . mean something?

RIG: You just remember that number, Sugar.

Pause. RIG *pulls out the front of* PHELONE's *shirt and peeks in.*

PHELONE: *(Moves closer to* RIG.*)* What are you doing?

RIG: *(Crossing to table.)* Checking your tits . . . *(Picks up knife.)*

PHELONE: It's breast cancer, not . . . tit cancer.

RIG: I'll cut them the fuck off. *(Pause. Holds out knife.)* You into knives?

PHELONE: *(Takes knife.)* I stare at my face on . . . the shiny part.

RIG: *(Crossing to door where Mom & Dad are stuffed.)* Oh yeah? *(Looks in room.)* Who, are they?

PHELONE: *(Crossing.)* Mother . . . and Dad.

RIG: They're fucking dead.

PHELONE: I had them stuffed. Mea paid for it. She pays for everything.

Pause.

RIG: Introduce me. Pretend I'm your fiancé.

PHELONE: Mom, Dad. This is, uhhh . . . *(Smiles.)* Rig . . . *(Whispers.)* What's your last name?

RIG: Mantes.

PHELONE: What's your middle name?

RIG: What's yours?

PHELONE: I don't have one. *(Pause.)* Rig . . . Mantes. We're getting married in a chapel. By . . . a justice of the peace. *(Crosses to table.)*

RIG: How did they die?

PHELONE *turns back.*

RIG: *(Crossing quickly.)* Answer my question!

PHELONE: *(Blurted out like a guilty child.)* My mother killed my dad and then, she killed herself.

RIG *sits on table.*

RIG: How'd she do it?

PHELONE: *(Entering kitchen.)* What?

RIG: Waste him.

PHELONE: Oh. She, gave him poison.

RIG: Hah.

PHELONE: *(Stands in entry.)* Then, she . . .

RIG: Wait! Don't tell me, Sugar. She took the rest herself.

Pause.

PHELONE: Want some tea?

Pause.

RIG: That's . . . perfect . . . *(Rises.)* Give me a teabag.

PHELONE: *(Holds up teabag.)* What for?

RIG: *(Holds out red gelcap.)* This.

PHELONE: What is it? *(Moves closer.)* Poison?

RIG: *(Grabs teabag.)* Heavy duty. . . . *(Bends over counter.)* Pay attention. . . . *(Opens teabag.)* Melts . . . in hot water. *(Hides gelcap in teabag.)* See . . . *(Puts teabag in box.)* There. *(Slides box away.)* Now, you keep it. *(Pause. Crosses to look at dead parents.)* I'll drink . . . tapwater.

PHELONE *crosses to stand in kitchen entry.*

PHELONE: Tell me, Rig . . . If, I got . . . this right. You want me to catch you . . . with your guard down.

RIG: That's the game, Sugar. *(Backing* PHELONE *into kitchen.)* I'll be your teacher.

PHELONE: Whatcha gonna teach me?

RIG: *(Pushes* PHELONE's *head below counter.)* Hey, Mom . . . Dad . . . *(Unzips fly.)* Guess who's coming . . . for dinner?

Blackout. Transcript tape begins. RIG *&* PHELONE *exit.*

Set change to MEA's *house.*

DARK
INTERLUDE:
Tape recording;
Wednesday Afternoon

SIDNEY: Well, Mr. Sontag . . . our time's about up.

SONTAG: Wait! I forgot. There's this voice in my head.

SIDNEY: When did it start?

SONTAG: Uhh . . . two months ago. That's why I came here.

SIDNEY: What kind of voice?

SONTAG: What kind?

SIDNEY: What does it sound like?

Pause.

SONTAG: "The William Tell Overture."

SIDNEY: You mean, it has words?

SONTAG: *(To music.) Tell . . . I'm Tell . . . I'm William Tell, I'm in your head . . . I'm in your head, I'm William Tell. . . . It's hell. . . . It's hell. . . . And now I'm going to make your life pure hell. . . . (Break.) You're all messed up . . . you've got problems . . . and you should see a therapist. . . . You're all messed . . .*

SIDNEY: Alright, Mr. Sontag . . . I get the picture. How often, does this voice occur?

SONTAG: I don't know. It . . . comes out of the blue. I tried listening to the music, but it only got worse. Should I come back next week?

SIDNEY: Well . . .

SONTAG: There are . . . other voices.

Tape of SONTAG *ends. Beep.*

SIDNEY: Patient Name: Mea Random . . . 4-2 . . . 96 . . . 1:20 p.m.

Tape ends. MEA *in place.*

SCENE 4

PART 1:
MEA's *house;*
Wednesday; Same Time

MEA *lies on couch. Remote sits on top of TV. Shorebreak sound begins.*

MEA: Darn . . . *(Sits up. Reaches under cushions.)* Where are you? *(Sees remote.)* Oh . . . *(Gets up.)* You old . . . fuddy duddy . . . *(Lies down. Clicks remote. Video begins.)*

During video, MEA *slowly becomes aware of her body.*

MADAME OVARY: Welcome to *Stalemate.* I'm Madam Ovary. I lost an ovary. I'm sure you have problems, too. Today, we welcome . . . Barry Chance and Jennifer . . . SooHaNaHeeNa. Did I say that right?

JENNIFER: Yes.

MADAME OVARY: From Phoenix, Arizona.

BARRY: Correct.

MADAME OVARY: And you are married to each other . . . platonically.

JENNIFER: We had sex once.

BARRY: Before we were married.

MADAME OVARY: Jennifer is a Native American rights activist, and Barry is . . . a professional gambler. So, what brought you two together?

JENNIFER: He wants to exploit the Navajo people.

BARRY: I keep telling her I'm gonna help them.

MADAME OVARY: This is *Stalemate.* *(Pause.)* Jennifer, what does "SooHaNaHeeNa" mean?

JENNIFER: Well, the literal translation from the Navajo language, is . . . "One Who at Least Sleeps Five Times a Day."

MADAME OVARY: That's quite a mouthful.

JENNIFER: I sleep a lot.

MADAME OVARY: Barry, how can you help the Indians?

BARRY: By building a five-star casino on their reservation.

JENNIFER: That land is sacred, Barry.

BARRY: By quadrupling their goverment subsidy.

JENNIFER: *(Pulls out black hairband with pink ears.)* He wants the women to walk around wearing these. *(Puts on hairband.)* It's degrading.

BARRY: Look, Jen. *(Pulls out colorful head dress.)* Lydia designed this. *(Puts on head dress.)* The ears are out.

MADAME OVARY: How did you two meet?

BARRY: Well, Madam Ovary . . . it's a funny story. I was scoping out some locations, you know, near this canyon . . . and there she was, dancing . . . with a flaming stick.

JENNIFER: It was a ritual, Barry, if you'd like to know. The Navajo people are running out of water.

BARRY: Their troubles are over. We're gonna pipe in water. More than they'll ever need.

JENNIFER: And just who is going to pipe in the water, Barry? You? . . . You can't even pay the cable bill on time.

BARRY: Hey, not so loud. I gotta deal with serious people.

JENNIFER: Yeah . . . five guys named Carmine.

MADAME OVARY: Come on, you two! Use that same energy to resolve your differences.

JENNIFER: How?

BARRY: You making fun?

JENNIFER: Huh?

BARRY: *(Holds up palm.)* How . . .

JENNIFER: That's not funny.

MADAME OVARY: What about . . . sex?

BARRY & JENNIFER: *(Same time.)* Uhhh . . .

MADAME OVARY: Try having it again.

BARRY: I get plenty in Vegas.
&
JENNIFER: I have an Indian lover.

MADAME OVARY: I think that now . . . would be the perfect time to . . . seek closure. Before it's too late.

BARRY: Okay, Madam Ovary. . . . When do we start?

MADAME OVARY: That's the healthy approach.

JENNIFER: I'm confused.

BARRY: Jeez!

MADAME OVARY: Why?

JENNIFER: Because . . . to the Navajo . . . There's no such thing as "closure." All life, good or bad . . . is "eternal."

MADAME OVARY: We'll be back . . . after this brief message.

MEA: *(Clicks remote.)* Hmm . . . *(TV off. Sighs. Stares at remote. Laughs.)* Back where you belong . . . *(Rises. Puts remote on top of TV as light fades. Shorebreak sound fades.* MEA *recorded tape begins.)*

SCENE 4

PART 2:
SIDNEY's office;
Same Time

Set change: To SIDNEY's *office.* SIDNEY *in place, evaluating recording of past session with* MEA.

SIDNEY: *(On tape.)* So . . . at the time . . . you, married his, partner . . .

MEA: I was twenty.

SIDNEY: You, remained . . . sexually active . . . with, your . . . father?

MEA: Yes.

SIDNEY: How often?

MEA: We had sex . . . the day he "died." *(Laughs.)*

SIDNEY: Why is that funny?

MEA: Had to be there, I guess . . .

SIDNEY: Then, take us back, Mea.

MEA: I can't. *(Pause.)* Don't you see. Right now . . . if I knew for certain that my father was waiting, I'd take one last bath.

Light rises on SIDNEY.

MEA: You know, nice and warm. Use the same knife, she did. *(Pause.)* Pretty twisted, huh? You're the only one I've told.

Pause on tape. Offstage, RIG *knocks twice on door.*

SIDNEY: *(On stage.)* Yes?

RIG: Doctor Merit.

SIDNEY: *(On tape.)* How'd it . . . *(Click.)*

SIDNEY: *(Stops tape.)* Yes.

RIG: Rig Mantes. *(Pause.)* Ring a bell, Doc. The "rapist." Remember?

Pause. SIDNEY *freezes.*

RIG: I think . . . *(Blackout.)* We need to talk.

Pause. Music rises. Close set. SIDNEY *exits.*

DARK

INTERMISSION

ACT II.

SCENE 1

PART 1:
SIDNEY's *office;* SIDNEY *&* RIG;
Same Wednesday; Ten Minutes Later

PART 2:
PHELONE's *house;* PHELONE *&* MEA;
Monday Afternoon; Five Days Later

DARK
INTERLUDE:
Telephone conversation; SIDNEY *&* FATHER;
Same; Twilight

SCENE 2

PART 1:
MEA's *house;* MEA *&* RIG;
Same; Twilight

PART 2:
SIDNEY's *office;* RIG;
Same; Three Hours Later

DARK
INTERLUDE:
RIG's *car;* RIG; *Driving to* PHELONE's *house;*
Same; Seven Minutes Later

SCENE 3

PART 1:
PHELONE's *house;* PHELONE *&* RIG;
Same; Thirty Minutes Later

PART 2:
SIDNEY's *office;* SIDNEY *&* MEA;
Tuesday Afternoon

DARK INTERLUDE:
Flashback; MEA's *car;* MEA *(driving) &* PHELONE
Early February; Same Year

SCENE 4

PART 1:
PHELONE's *house;* PHELONE *&* RIG;
Same Time

FAST FORWARD:
Voicemail message; PHELONE;
Two Months Later

PART 2:
SIDNEY's *office;* SIDNEY;
One Month Later

ACT II.

SCENE 1

PART 1:
SIDNEY's *office;*
Same Wednesday; Ten Minutes Later

Open set. SIDNEY *(SL standing) &* RIG *(in* MEA's *chair, legs spread out) in place. Music fades.*

RIG: Is this how they sit?

SIDNEY: Who?

Light fades up.

RIG: Your clients.

SIDNEY: They vary.

RIG: *(Rises. Crossing to* SIDNEY's *chair.)* And this must be . . . the vantage point. . . . *(Sits.)* Relax. . . . Enjoy the pain.

SIDNEY: How long were you camped outside my office? *(Crosses behind* RIG.*)* What mask did you use on Mea?

Pause.

RIG: *(Rises.)* Don't stroke me, Doc. *(Crosses to* MEA's *chair.)* This chair's better. *(Lies face down. Starts humping chair. Turns over laughing.)*

SIDNEY: I can't believe they let you out.

RIG: Here I am . . .

SIDNEY: And why is that?

RIG: When I left Soledad, three weeks ago . . . I walked through a field with no walls. *(Pause.)* And when I closed my eyes . . . your face was the first I saw.

SIDNEY: What about the girl you beat to a pulp?

RIG: She's part of me, too. *(Rises. Points to* MEA's *chair.)* Care to sit?

SIDNEY: They'll get you back, if . . . in any way you hurt Mea Random.

RIG: Put it in writing?

SIDNEY: I won't let you down.

RIG: You owe me two years already.

Pause.

SIDNEY: *(Sits.)* Correct me if I'm wrong. But I seem . . . to remember your father killed your mother, right?

RIG: Close. Only crippled her . . .

SIDNEY: *(Looks at watch.)* I have an appointment.

RIG: *(Settling back.)* She died a year later . . .

SIDNEY: Are you comfortable at Mea's?

RIG: Yes I am . . . and thanks for asking. I'm doing the sister, too.

SIDNEY: Phelone?

RIG: Uh huh.

SIDNEY: Did she . . . Does Mea know?

RIG: I get it . . . *(Pause.)* You're hot for the Youngblood. *(Rises.)* No big deal. Tell me when, if you want. I'll bring her over . . . *(Crosses.)* You really fucked me that time with your parole report. *(Sticks out hand.)*

SIDNEY: *(Hesitates; shakes hand.)* See you.

RIG: Count on it.

Sidney drops RIG's *hand. Rig crosses to doorway.*

SIDNEY: Watch out for Mea.

Light begins to fade.

RIG: You and me both, Doc. *(Stops in doorway.)* There's no place like hell.

Light out. Silence. Recording begins. SIDNEY & RIG *exit.*

SCENE 1

PART 2 :
PHELONE's *house;*
Monday Afternoon; Five Days Later

Set change: SIDNEY's *office to* PHELONE's *house.* PHELONE & MEA *in place.*

PHELONE: *(Recording.)* You think Mea knows . . . about lesbians? The one on TV . . . was just like me. She said men didn't want her, so . . . she tried woman. And lived happily ever after. I wonder what they feel like. You think, Mea knows? *(Pause.)* Lately . . . I dream about poison. Poison. Everything's poison. Even Mother and Dad. What about the man you met? What about Rig? I don't know. Did he, have a hard on? Daddy does. Daddy, Daddy, Daddy. Next time, I want to have a woman. How old? Older than me. What color hair? Blonde. Not because, they have more fun. Then, why? Because Mother was a blonde. *(Pause.)* Here comes, Mea. . . . Come in.

Recording ends.

MEA: *(Crossing* CS, *carries grocery bag to kitchen.)* Hiya, hiya.

PHELONE: *(Follows.)* What'd you bring?

Light rises.

MEA: *(Setting bag down.)* Some snacks.

PHELONE: *(Grabbing bag.)* Sugar! *(Pause. Looks in bag.)* These are my favorite. Have I ever had them? *(MEA exits kitchen.)* Look!

MEA: Hello, Mom. Dad.

PHELONE: You're the greatest sister, Mea.

MEA: *(Sits. Aside.)* Also . . . the last.

PHELONE *exits kitchen & crosses* CS, *chewing red licorice.*

PHELONE: *(Posing.)* Right on. . . . Right on.

MEA: What are you doing?

PHELONE: *(Changes pose.)* Having a cool, cool time. Some show last night on cable. *(Changes pose.)* Did you see it?

MEA: No. What channel?

PHELONE: Eighty-seven. Right on . . . about the . . . so-ci-al *(so-she-ul)*

MEA: —Pa-thic?

PHELONE: *(Shakes head.)* Sociological. Impact of slang in America. *The Autobiography of* . . . *(Changes pose.)* "*Right On.*" Right on . . . Right on. It started in the sixties with, you know . . . Pink Panthers. . . . *(Pause.* PHELONE *waits.* MEA *doesn't correct her.)* It meant . . . *(Raises fist.)* We're brothers—Right on. It became more cautious, in the seventies. . . . They're out to get us—Right on. Doctors in the eighties used it on the golf course. . . . Nice shot. Hole in one. Right on. And then, in the nineties . . . it meant, I agree . . . I don't have to consult my therapist—Right on. . . . Right on.

MEA: How do you fit all that up there?

PHELONE: It's important.

MEA: What day is it?

PHELONE: *(Crossing* USR; *sets licorice down in kitchen.)* Uhh . . . Let's see . . . you're here . . . must be Monday. *(Sits.)* Talked to Dad, this morning.

MEA: Did you?

Pause.

PHELONE: He forgave me. Said, "How's my baby kitten?" I said, "Fine, Daddy. Would you like . . . to talk to yourself?" . . . He laughed. *(Pause.)* Remember his laugh? Then, he asked . . . "How's my other Sugar?" I said . . .

MEA: Sugar? *(Pause.)* He never called me that.

PHELONE: *(Rising.)* Maybe it wasn't him. *(Enters kitchen.)* Sure sounded like Dad. *(Pause. Crossing back.)* I ran out of raisins. *(Sits.)*

MEA: So. You met Rig.

PHELONE: Did I?

MEA: When?

PHELONE: He came over.

MEA: Last week?

PHELONE: Uh huh . . .

MEA: How long did he stay?

PHELONE: You didn't tell me . . . you had a boyfriend. *(Pause.)* Don't worry. I told Mom and Dad. . . .

MEA: What did he want?

PHELONE: I called your house. He answered. You were with Sidney.

MEA: That's all?

PHELONE: That's all. *(Pause.)* Isn't Rig a funny name?

MEA *pats* PHELONE's *head.* PHELONE *pants like a dog. They laugh.*

MEA: See, his name was Rick . . . but he changed it to Rig . . .

PHELONE: Why come?

MEA: Cause they . . . made fun of it at school . . . you know, called him Dick.

PHELONE: Ohhh . . .

MEA *touches* PHELONE's *hair. Light begins to fade.*

MEA: One day this week . . . we'll go and see Barbara. She'll . . . fix your hair. . . .

PHELONE: Do my nails?

MEA: And do your nails. . . .

PHELONE: What color?

Pause.

MEA: Whatever you want.

Light out. Recording begins. MEA *&* PHELONE *exit. Set change to* MEA's *house.*

DARK
INTERLUDE:
Telephone conversation;
Same; Twilight

SIDNEY: I forgot what I wanted to ask you, Dad.

FATHER: Short term memory's the first to go.

SIDNEY: Where does it go?

FATHER: You're forty now, Sid. There are ways to put things—not wheres. *(Pause.)* How's business?

SIDNEY: Keeping up with their jones.

FATHER: *(Laughs.)* Very funny, Daughter Merit.

SIDNEY: Off the top of my head.

FATHER: And what about your own?

Pause.

SIDNEY: It's . . . under control.

FATHER: Good.

SIDNEY: How's research?

FATHER: Funds are drying up.

SIDNEY: Election year.

FATHER: Don't I know. Look, Sid. I'll be home next week. Call you Monday, as always . . . *(Click.)*

SIDNEY: Bye. *(Click.)*

End recording. RIG *in place on couch.*

SCENE 2

PART 1:
MEA's *house;*
Same; Twilight

Shorebreak sound rises. Twilight rises in window. MEA *crosses* SR. *Light fades throughout scene. Seeing* RIG, MEA *stops.*

MEA: I knew you were there . . . Rig.

RIG: I like the dark, Sugar.

MEA: Where's your car?

RIG: Down the street. I'm going out for a while.

MEA: Coming back?

RIG: Maybe later. . . . How's your sister?

MEA: Fine. . . . *(Sitting.)* Heard you got together. . . .

RIG: That we did.

MEA: You should've told me.

RIG: Shoulda-woulda . . . like, you coulda . . . told her about me, Sugar. . . . *(Pause.)* You made what goes come around to this.

MEA: I don't park my car down the street.

RIG: That bother you? It's nothing.

MEA: Sneaking around behind my back I don't think of . . . as nothing.

RIG: She called. . . . You were out.

MEA: I was at the—with Sidney.

RIG: Cut the charade, Sugar . . . I know her, too.

MEA: Sidney Merit . . .

RIG: Doc-tor Merit. Me and her go way back.

MEA: Were you a patient?

RIG: I was a convict.

MEA: In prison?

RIG: State prison. Soledad, Sugar.

MEA: What crime did you commit?

RIG: What do you think?

MEA: *(Hesitates.)* Uhhhh . . . rape.

RIG: It's almost dark. . . .

Pause.

RIG: What'd you pay, to stuff them?

MEA *frowns.*

RIG: She asked me over.

MEA *relaxes.*

RIG: You're a funny bird . . .

MEA: How long were you in?

Pause.

RIG: Six years.

MEA: That's a long time . . .

RIG: Plenty of it, Sugar.

MEA: So, she went there, what? To study you, or something?

RIG: I was her project, two years ago.

Pause.

MEA: I don't get it. . . .

RIG: She's smarter than you think.

MEA: Who?

RIG: Your sister. She's strong. . . .

Pause. Light's just about faded.

MEA: Will she get hurt?

RIG: Well, I figure . . . life wouldn't be much . . . without pain, now, would it? Don't worry. She'll come out alright.

MEA: Promise?

RIG: Till death, Mea. . . .

MEA: That's all I want.

RIG: Me, too . . . see . . . it's a package deal.

Light out.

RIG: We . . . all get . . . what we want.

Tape begins. Set changes to SIDNEY's *office.* MEA *exits.* RIG *in place.*

SCENE 2

PART 2:
SIDNEY's *office;*
Same; Three Hours Later

RIG *sits in* SIDNEY's *chair listening to* MEA *recordings.*

SIDNEY: *(Recording.)* Patient name: Mea Random . . . 6-18-___ *(use year of production)* . . . 1:23 p.m.

RIG *fast forwards tape (recording).*

MEA: I don't feel anything. I can't feel anything.

SIDNEY: You feel love for your sister. . . .

MEA: I'm afraid of her.

RIG *fast forwards recording.*

MEA: The first doctor, I had . . . right after they "died" . . . became obsessed with me.

SIDNEY: How?

MEA: We had an affair. Well, I wouldn't call it that.

SIDNEY: Why?

MEA: Because she was a woman, too.

RIG *fast forwards recording.*

MEA: I remember it all like yesterday. Dad in the tub. Phelone watching TV.

RIG: *(On stage.)* This is the one. . . .

Light rises. RIG *sinks back in chair.*

MEA: *(Recording.)* Mother was in the kitchen, humming . . . What was the song? . . . "Somewhere, My Love" . . . cutting onions, carrots, and celery. I asked her what she was making. She didn't answer. Dad started screaming. I ran to the bathroom. The water around him, was violet in color. I don't know what made her do it, but Phelone snapped. His last word was "no." . . . There was a knife sticking out of him. She had stabbed him, all over. I threw up in the toilet.

Pause.

RIG: You must love this shit, don't you? . . .

MEA: *(Recording.)* Phelone was splashing her hand in the water. When, I finished . . . I saw mother looking in . . . her face seemed, so calm. She wandered off. I followed her into the garage. She grabbed a box of something off the shelf above the tools . . . and went back to the kitchen. I just stood there . . . lifeless. Phelone was dancing around the dining room table. Mother drank the poison.

Pause.

RIG: *(Turns off machine. Rises.)* Well, Youngblood . . . it's time to play. . . .

RIG *crosses to exit. Light fades. Tape begins.* RIG *exits.*

Set changes to PHELONE's *house.*

DARK
INTERLUDE:
RIG's *car; Driving to* PHELONE's *house;*
Same; Seven Minutes Later

Sound of traffic in background.

RIG: Show and tell, little girl . . . and, Sugar, too. I'm coming. It's coming. Need a little music, now . . . to soothe the beast within . . .

RIG *turns on radio. Froth music begins. TV moves* CS. PHELONE *in place (on floor).*

SCENE 3:

PART 1
PHELONE's *house;*
Same; Thirty Minutes Later

Light rises. TV monitor on CS. *Video begins. Same froth music comes from TV.* PHELONE *lies onstage facing TV.* GET WELL GURU *appears (on screen) walking down rooming house hallway.*

PHELONE: It's *Get Well Guru* . . .

Onscreen DEATH WISHETTE *appears behind* GET WELL GURU.

PHELONE: And Death Wishette. . . .

GURU *&* WISHETTE *close in to hover in front of camera. Cut to* GURU *dressed in business suit.*

GURU: This is . . . *Atrophy.*

DEATH WISHETTE: *Atrophy.* . . .

GURU: For you morons . . . that means . . . failure to evolve because of insufficient nutrition. . . .

DEATH WISHETTE: We're your nutrition.

GURU: *(Pointing.)* Death Wishette . . .

DEATH WISHETTE: *(Pointing.)* And, Get Well Guru.

Cut to GURU *lying on couch holding trophy with baby nipple on end.*

GURU: Atrophy . . . could be . . . A trophy . . . like this . . . *(Sucks on nipple.)* Ma-ma . . . Ma-ma . . .

DEATH WISHETTE: *(Rises from behind couch.)* Look at me, look at me, look at me, look at me. . . .

GURU: That's right, Death Wishette. *(Holds out trophy.)* Get a trophy. . . . Want another.

DEATH WISHETTE: Just one more, please. . . . Just one more, please. . . .

GURU: Lack of nutrition . . . *(Hurls trophy at camera. Cut to test pattern.)* This is only a test. . . .

Cut to GURU *(from torso up) nailed to cross. Close in on right hand dripping blood. Cut to* DEATH WISHETTE *catching drops of blood in her mouth.*

DEATH WISHETTE: *(Smiles.)* Even Jesus turned to violence. . . .

Cut to light show. Music rises. Cut to GURU.

GURU: Tell 'em about the Death Wish, Ette.

Music fades. DEATH WISHETTE *enters frame.* GURU *backs out.*

RIG *enters & leans against wall watching* PHELONE *stare at TV.*

DEATH WISHETTE: Listen, boys and girls. . . . The "Wish" is built in. So, deal with it. Manipulate. You're gonna die, too . . . whether you want to, or not. . . . So, don't take your own life. . . . Take advantage of others. . . . *(Pause.)*

RIG *yanks plug from wall screen goes blank.*

PHELONE: Hey . . .

RIG: *(Rising.)* Hey, yourself . . . *(Crosses* DSR.*)*

PHELONE: Where's Mea?

RIG: Home, sleeping . . . *(Pushes TV back.)*

PHELONE *rolls over.*

RIG: *(Turns.)* Know why I came back?

PHELONE: You couldn't live without me.

RIG: *(Squatting.)* Close, Sugar . . . Close. One word off.

PHELONE: *(Rises dancing.)* Rig's got a death wish . . .

RIG: Act your age . . .

PHELONE: Wanna fuck? *(Pause.)* I know a secret. Your name was Rick. But you changed it to Rig. So now, I think . . . I'll call you Twig. *(Dancing around.)* Rig the Twig . . . Rig the Twig . . .

RIG *attacks* PHELONE *& throws her to the floor.*

RIG: *(Slaps* PHELONE *three times back and forth.)* I'll teach you! I'll teach you! I'll teach you! *(Holds closed right fist above* PHELONE.*)* Fuuuuuck! You're twenty-four . . . I'll break twenty-four bones in your motherfuckin' body!

PHELONE: *(Calmly.)* You're five years old. . . . You eat five bites of peas. . . .

RIG *rolls off* PHELONE SR *by* DAD's *leg.* PHELONE *crawls toward* RIG. RIG *touches* DAD's *pants cuff.* PHELONE *puts her head on* RIG's *lap. Pause. Light softens.*

PHELONE: What kind of poison is that, you gave me?

RIG: Deadly, Sugar. Like a lethal injection. I got it from a guy in prison.

PHELONE: Why didn't you take it anyway, I mean . . . if you wanna die?

Pause.

RIG: It ain't that easy. . . .

Pause.

PHELONE: How'd you get in my house?

RIG: I got the key. *(Pause.)* Your sister told me everything. . . .

Light fades. Recording of MEA's *phone message to* PHELONE *plays.* PHELONE *&* RIG *exit.*

Set change to SIDNEY's *office.* SIDNEY *&* MEA *in place.*

PHELONE'S PHONE MESSAGE: Whoever you are, you have the wrong number . . . except Mea. Mea . . . please leave a message . . . By the way, it's Phelone Random . . .

(Beep.)

MEA: *(On tape.)* Wake up. . . . It's past noon. Pick up the phone. Is Rig over there? . . . He never came home. Okay, okay . . . I'm off to Sidney's. I'll call you later. . . . Better still, I'll come by. . . . *(Pause. Click.)*

RIG: *(On tape—hums.) Somewhere . . . My Love . . . There will be songs to sing . . .*

Tape ends.

SCENE 3

PART 2:
SIDNEY's *office;*
Tuesday Afternoon

MEA: You mean, here? Last night? . . . Why would he do that?

Pause. Light rises.

SIDNEY: To find out about you.

MEA: Then he heard everything . . .

SIDNEY: We'll have to go with that assumption.

MEA: It's funny, I . . . feel free now . . .

SIDNEY: It wasn't your office.

MEA: Right. . . . Right. . . . Did he really rape someone?

SIDNEY: No.

MEA: I thought so. . . .

SIDNEY: Much worse.

MEA: Oh . . .

SIDNEY: *(Removes file.)* Listen, Mea. . . . *(Opens file—reads.)* he almost killed a girl . . . about your sister's age. Brutal assault. She was never the same. Convicted of rape the following year. Spent six years . . .

MEA: He told me . . .

SIDNEY: He told you?

MEA: Soledad. *(Pause.)* He also said . . . he met you there.

SIDNEY: I went to observe him. The man is dangerous.

MEA: Why was he waiting, outside your office?

SIDNEY: Motivation . . .

MEA: To hurt you?

SIDNEY: To hurt himself . . . See, Rig has what we call . . . the death instinct. Self-destructive behavior . . . in the form of aggression toward others.

Pause.

MEA: Compared to Rig . . . how would you categorize me?

SIDNEY: Outwardly cathartic . . . but very much alike.

SIDNEY *turns off recording device. Light begins to fade.*

SIDNEY: So, you think he's with your sister?

MEA: She didn't answer the phone.

SIDNEY: You going over?

MEA: I have to.

SIDNEY: I wouldn't advise it.

MEA: You can't undo, Sidney . . . what's already been done.

Light fades. Recording begins. Set change to PHELONE's *house.* SIDNEY *&*
MEA *exit.*

DARK
INTERLUDE:
Flashback; MEA's *car;*
Early February; Same Year

PHELONE: You like the new doctor?

MEA: I believe so . . .

PHELONE: What's her name?

MEA: Sidney Merit . . .

Pause.

PHELONE: What happened with . . . the last doctor?

Long pause.

PHELONE: Where we going? There's Pink's. Didn't we go there once?
I had a big chili dog. . . .

MEA: Will you be quiet for just one minute?

PHELONE: Where we going?

Pause.

PHELONE: So, you like the doctor?

MEA: Yes! Yes! Stop bothering me!

PHELONE: My birthday's next week.

MEA: I know.

PHELONE: Did I give you any hints?

MEA: Plenty. . . .

PHELONE: Forget the plates . . . I don't want plates. I'd like one of
those blow up men dolls. . . .

End flashback.

SCENE 4

PART 1:
PHELONE's *house:*
Same Time

PHELONE: *(Standing in doorway of family room holding cable guide.)*
Mommy . . . Daddy. Whatcha wanna watch today? *(Thumbs
through.)* Let's see . . .

RIG *enters* SR *in underwear.*

RIG: *(Peeks in.)* How about The Fuck Channel?

PHELONE: They never fuck.

RIG: They had to once.

PHELONE: Hey! What about me?

Pause.

RIG: You're Mea's daughter. . . .

PHELONE: She couldn't have me at seven.

RIG: *(Rubs against* PHELONE.*)* There's seven again, Youngblood.

PHELONE: *(Holds her nose.)* You need a shower.

RIG: I'm taking . . . a bath.

Rig turns. MEA *enters.*

PHELONE: Hi, Mea.

RIG: *(Kissing* MEA's *cheek)* 'Lo, Sugar.

MEA: *(Crosses.)* What the hell is going on?

Pause.

PHELONE: *(Crossing to table.)* Rig's gonna take a bath. . . .

RIG: That's right, Sugar. . . . Youngblood thinks I smell bad.

PHELONE: *(Sits.)* He knows I killed Dad.

RIG: I won't be long. . . . *(Exits.)*

MEA: Something's missing. . . .

PHELONE: What?

MEA: The sound . . .

PHELONE: Huh . . .

MEA: The sound of his walk. You know . . . click-click-click.

RIG: *(Offstage.)* I can hear you, Sugar . . . *(Pause. Enters with shoes on. Stops* SR *of table.)* Know why, I walk like that?

MEA *&* PHELONE *shake their heads no.*

RIG: 'Cause that's how the guards in the joint do it. *(Exits.)*

PHELONE: *(Whispers.)* He told me he was in prison. *(Short pause. Excited.)* I remember what I wanted to ask you, from yesterday, Mea. Do you know anything about lesbians?

Pause.

RIG: *(Offstage.)* Better answer.

PHELONE: I saw one on TV.

RIG: *(Offstage.)* Tell her about the first doctor.

PHELONE: Men didn't want her.

MEA *enters kitchen and stares out through counter.*

RIG: *(Offstage.)* You hear me?

PHELONE: What's his problem?

RIG: *(Offstage.)* When I get out . . . your sister's gonna show you what a lesbian is. . . .

Pause. MEA *drifts.* RIG *hums, "Somewhere, My Love."* PHELONE *rises, crossing* DSR, *and unplugs extension cord from wall, then TV.* PHELONE *drops cord* CS *and crosses* DS *to counter.*

PHELONE: Let me have a knife, please.

MEA, *not thinking, hands knife through counter.* PHELONE *takes it, returns* CS, *and sitting, begins fraying one end of the cord.*

RIG *continues to hum.*

MEA: *(Snaps back.)* Phelone! *(Exits kitchen.)* What for?

PHELONE: I'm playing a game.

MEA: *(Relieved; returning to kitchen.)* Remember the time, at the beach in Del Mar? . . . (PHELONE *doesn't answer.)* We thought Dad drowned, but he was only fooling. . . . Remember? . . .

RIG: *(Offstage.)* Hey, Youngblood . . . bring me a towel.

PHELONE *rises & sticks plug back in, holding frayed end in other hand.*

MEA: He disappeared in the water, and we started screaming. . . .

RIG: *(Offstage.)* Where's the fucking towel!

PHELONE *exits* SL, *calmly with cord in hand.*

MEA: He snuck up behind us . . .

RIG: *(Offstage.)* Look, you little cunt, I want . . .

PHELONE *(Offstage.) drops cord in tub.*

RIG: SSSSSSZZZZZZZZZZZZZZ.

MEA *leaves kitchen.* PHELONE *enters.*

MEA: What's that noise? *(Exits* SL.*)*

PHELONE *enters kitchen and puts teapot on stove.*

MEA: *(Offstage.)* Oh, my God! Oh, my God! . . .

PHELONE *leaves kitchen.* MEA *enters.*

MEA: What happened?

PHELONE: *(Unplugs cord.)* He's dead.

MEA: I was fourteen. . . . *(Crossing.)* You were only seven. . . . *(Sits.)*

PHELONE *unplugs cord and rolls it up methodically. She crosses to family room and drops cord at Dad's foot.*

MEA: We were so happy. . . .

PHELONE *enters kitchen, places cup on counter, takes out poison teabag, places it in cup, grabs teapot, and pours water into cup. She dunks teabag twice, throws out teabag, and exits kitchen.*

PHELONE: *(SL to MEA.)* When Father died . . . Mother drank tea. . . .

MEA *looks at cup. Long pause.* MEA *enters kitchen.* PHELONE *backs up two steps.* MEA *stands in front of cup. Long pause.*

MEA *stares at* PHELONE. *Long pause.*

MEA *drinks tea and sets down cup.* MEA *turns pale and laughs, then dies. Her right foot shows through kitchen doorway.*

PHELONE *sinks to her knees, takes a deep breath, holds it, and lies face out (hand to head; elbow to stage) on her right side. Long pause.*

PHELONE *exhales and rolls on her back. Pause. Light begins to fade.*

PHELONE: At least I know . . . what a man feels like. . . .

Light fades. Tape begins. Set change to SIDNEY's *office.*
PHELONE *&* MEA *exit.*

SCENE 4

FAST FORWARD:
Voicemail message;
Two Months Later

SIDNEY'S MESSAGE: This is the office of . . . Sidney Merit. Please wait
. . . before starting your message . . . for the series of beeps
. . . to end. . . . *(Four beeps.)*

PHELONE'S MESSAGE: *(Faint doll house music in background.)* Hello,
Sidney . . . It's Phelone Random. I just called, I . . . wanted to
thank you for everything . . . that, you know, you've done. . . .
(Pause.) I took Mea out to Catalina. . . . Her ashes. I couldn't
believe there were quite so many. It was windy, but pleasant. . . . I
ate lunch on the island. . . . I'm sorry things ended, the way they
did. . . . *(Pause. Shorebreak recording rises. Doll music fades.)* The house
is for sale. . . . I moved into Mea's. I never realized how much I
like the sound of the ocean. Now I live by it. . . . I'm taking driving
lessons. . . . *(Pause.)* One more thing. . . . *(Pause.)* Thanks for not
telling. . . . *(Click.)*

Tape ends. SIDNEY *in place.*

SCENE 4

PART 2:
SIDNEY'*s office;*
One Month Later

SIDNEY: *(Paper in hand, reads referral.)* Here are the subjects, with
which William needs to deal. *(Pause. Light rises.)* I've discussed
them with him and he seeks your help. One . . . he seems to end
up on the outside of relationships. He dates very nice, young
ladies, but . . . it never works out. Two . . . William experiences fits
of depression. . . .

PHELONE *knocks twice on door*

SIDNEY: Yes? . . .

PHELONE: *(Offstage.)* Open up . . . It's Mea. . . .

SIDNEY *turns recorder on.*

SIDNEY: Wait. . . .

SIDNEY *grabs microphone.*

SIDNEY: *(Into microphone.)* Patient Name: Mea Random. . . . 10-1-__
   (use year of production) . . . 1:18 p.m. . . .

SIDNEY *hides microphone on second shelf. Light fades, except for anteroom.*

Pause. Pinpoint spot remains on doorknob only.

PHELONE (MEA): *(Offstage.)* I'm waiting. . . .

Blackout.

THE END

INSIDE STRAIGHT

STRAIGHT

A PLAY BY
PETER CARLAFTES

PRODUCTION NOTES:

Inside Straight was a love letter to San Francisco and Neil Simon. As corny as Neil Simon might seem to some, even in his own time, there was a true depth of humor that I instilled in the writing from the start. And while bachelors and newlyweds and divorcees had found their own voices through the comedies of Simon, the gay and lesbian cultures seemed limited to campy romps or emotional rescues from other playwrights. So I dug into two relationships—the first, two men; the second, two women—and discovered a common thread of "luck-drawn love" and "moments between" that brought them together, then drove them apart. And astonishingly, the humor shone through. Promise fulfilled.

For the set, after much thought before the original production, I decided to cut up the furniture—leaving smaller pieces of the whole in place on the stage to illustrate to the audience that something was missing. This idea worked in the small confines of Marilyn Monroe Memorial Theater, but I believe this course of action would restrict the impact of the play's comic moments in a larger house.

—*P. C.*

INSIDE
STRAIGHT

PLAY:
*Poker term for hand that draws
the card it needs to be complete*

PLACE:
San Francisco

PROMISE:
Preoccupy love

CREATION:

LENA: *Twenty-five-year-old musician and performance artist; paradoxically on the verge of the American Dream; lives with* MEREDITH; *plays drums with The Objects*

RICKY: *Thirty-year-old part-time flight attendant; lives with* ANTOINE; *bit of a playboy; unnerved by the fact that he likes being kept*

MEREDITH: *Thirty-five-year-old booking agent slash talent scout;* LENA's *mentor and lover; a self-made brillo pad wearing out*

ANTOINE: *Forty-year-old first-class master chef and restaurant owner;* RICKY's *lover; thrives on immediacy; demands attention by courting disaster*

OPENING ONE:
RICKY *in bed; morning*

OPENING TWO:
LENA *in bed; morning*

SEGUE ONE:
RICKY & LENA; *bar; that afternoon*

SCENE ONE:
ANTOINE & RICKY; *bedroom; late same afternoon*

SCENE TWO:
MEREDITH & LENA; *living room; late same afternoon*

FLASHBACK:
LENA, MEREDITH, ANTOINE & RICKY;
dressing room at the Cat O' Nine Tales; six months earlier

SEGUE TWO:
LENA & RICKY; *bar; two weeks from Segue One*

SCENE THREE:
LENA, MEREDITH, ANTOINE & RICKY;
living room; one month later

SCENE FOUR:
RICKY *and* ANTOINE; *bedroom; two weeks later*

SEGUE THREE:
ANTOINE & MEREDITH; *bar; one month later*

FINALE:
RICKY & LENA; *home; same time*

PRELUDE

classical romance music
(Gershwin, Previn—perhaps live)
sets mood before play begins

STAGE:

ACT I.

OPENING ONE:
RICKY *in bed; morning*

Stage lights off; bed lowers back wall CS. RICKY *in place—head downstage.*
ANTOINE *(on phone) in place* SL. *Music fades. Lights up to dawn.*

ANTOINE: *(Pacing* SL *talking as quietly as* ANTOINE *can on cell/Bluetooth)*
What do you mean "A Tarantula!" Like a big fat hairy spider!
How could the San Francisco Opera do this to me? It'll ruin
everything—what? . . . Not "A" Tarantula, "The" Tarantula? . . .
It's the ship from Pirates of Penzance . . . ahhh—so your ice
sculpting fits with my nautical theme. . . . What a relief! *(RICKY
stirs slightly.)* And you will personally deliver it to the terrace of
the Opera House by 3 p.m.? . . . Perfect. I'm glad you're happy
they gave you your big chance. Yes. Bye now. *(End phone call.)*
Oh—sorry, Ricky. Did I just wake you?

RICKY: *(Turns over on left side.)* No, Antoine. You did that three
hours ago.

ANTOINE: What do you mean? How?

RICKY: Talking in your sleep.

ANTOINE: Well it IS my big night!

RICKY: I know. That's what you kept saying. It's my Big Night! It's my Big Night! Over and over.

ANTOINE: *(Dials cell.)* I've got to talk to Ken. Do you have any plans today?

RICKY: *(Turning back on back.)* Outside of listening to you say, "It's my big night?"

ANTOINE: *(Talks over* RICKY *to phone.)* Hi, Ken, yes—good morning to you, too. Yes, it is early.

RICKY: Maybe walk over to the Haight.

ANTOINE: Ken? Please go on receive.

RICKY: Do a little shopping.

ANTOINE: Before you do anything else—strain the shells from the big pot, stir in the cream and then just let it simmer. *(To* RICKY.*)* You'll be home by four? Tonight's my big night!

RICKY: *(Turns on right side.)* Wouldn't miss it for the world.

ANTOINE: *(To phone.)* Stop it, Beast—I was talking to Ricky . . . I'll be there in twenty minutes. And don't forget to roll the hors d'oeuvre trays out of the walk-in now and let them thaw somewhere out of the way. . . .*(Lights fade.)* What do you mean there is no place left that's out of the way. Don't argue with me, Ken! You know perfectly well that. . . . *(Antoine fades conversation.)*

Piano music fades up with conversation out. RICKY *&* ANTOINE *offstage.*

LENA *in place on bed—head downstage same as* RICKY. MEREDITH *in place* SR.

OPENING TWO:
LENA *in bed; morning*

MEREDITH *paces* SR *talking to cellphone via Bluetooth. Piano music fades with* MEREDITH *conversation rising). Lights up. Same dawn—different direction.*

MEREDITH: *(As if to a child.)* Please stop talking, Ben, and think about climbing into bed and closing your eyes. Remember sleep, Ben? You have to get some. . . . *(Pause. Hardens.)* How the hell do you think you're going to make it to your gig tonight, Ben—if you're passed out on the floor? *(LENA stirs slightly.)* You're on the floor now snorting what? I don't even know what that is. . . . Well, I'm sorry you're out, Ben—but this could be a good thing. See the positive. . . . *(LENA turns over on her right side facing MEREDITH.)* No, Ben—don't you see that getting more is a negative? You play in a band with three other members. You are the front man. Gentleman Ben. They are counting on you.

LENA: Yeah, right. They're probably counting on him to bring them some.

MEREDITH: *(Chuckles.)* No, Ben—I'm not laughing at you. Yes— I promise. Don't get paranoid, Ben. Get some sleep.

LENA: You're up early.

MEREDITH: *(Puts phone on mute.)* Goddamn Gentleman Ben is driving me nuts. *(Sits on edge of bed.)* Sorry to wake you.

LENA: *(Touches MEREDITH's back.)* Well I did leave my door open. *(Turns over on back.)*

MEREDITH: *(Catches on. Stares at LENA. Long pause. Takes phone off mute.)* Are you there, Ben? What happened? *(Standing.)* I hear snoring. Ben! Ben! What a break! He passed out. *(Hangs up.)* Let's hope he makes the gig. *("Where-were-we?" short pause. The moment's gone.)* Any plans today, Lena?

LENA: *(Turns over on left side.)* Not anymore. *(Short pause.)* Maybe walk up to the Haight later.

MEREDITH: Shit! *(Dialing phone.)* I've got to call New York! Almost forgot. That's why I got up in the first place. Yes—I'd like to speak with Fizzy . . . Meredith Kinkaid, SF Bandwidth. . . . This is in reference to Bozo the Noun. . . .

LENA: *(Under breath.)* They only use nouns.

MEREDITH: *(To* LENA.*)* They only use nouns in their lyrics. What a concept! They're gonna be big—not as big as your band, but . . . Let me get out of here. Go back to sleep. *(Closes door leaving* LENA's *room.)* Sorry.

LENA: Me, too.

MEREDITH: Hello, Fizzy. . . . Who's this?. . . Not Fizzy. Cute. Look. I'd like to discuss booking Bozo the Noun for a west coast tour, not your first day of Pre-K, hon. So let me talk to Fizzy . . . *(Lights fade.)* Now!

(Techno beat up.)

SEGUE ONE:
RICKY *&* LENA; *bar; that afternoon*

SYNTHESIS:
Bed up, bar opens; music mixes into a techno beat; table and chairs already in place; LENA *sits* SL; RICKY SR; *the two are joined in mid-conversation; prelude fades out; bar lights rise up as* RICKY *begins. Bar music fades.*

RICKY: I don't know why—it's crazy, Lena . . . I mean, you know Antoine. . . . He gets better with age. . . . It's . . . just . . . sometimes I feel more like a lap dog than his lover.

LENA *smiles softly, staring somewhere else.*

RICKY: As she sits here smiling. Why are you smiling?

LENA: Mmm, nothing . . . it's sweet.

RICKY: What? . . . Being a pet?

LENA: Well, yeah . . . not you, but . . . being a pet.

Pause.

LENA: Being someone's creation.

RICKY: Don't tell me. . . . You had this dog when you were little . . . that always understood every word you said. . . .

LENA: Funny . . . from what . . . how an image comes along. . . . Me? No—I'm not . . . ready for a dog.

RICKY: Maybe down the road . . .

LENA: Could be . . .

RICKY: Who knows . . .

LENA: Time's hard to figure . . .

RICKY: Maybe when you're thirty . . .

LENA: What the hell's thirty got to do with* some dog?

RICKY: Hey*, anything's possible. . . .

RICKY's "hey" on LENA's "with"

LENA: So . . .

RICKY: Look!

LENA: At what?

RICKY: *(Plays fortune teller.)* Silence!

LENA: Huh?

RICKY: *(Rubbing crystal ball.)* Look, Lena. . . . Wait! . . .

LENA: *(Catches on.)* I'm waiting . . .

RICKY: Look down the road . . .

LENA: Oh, great shaman . . . can I gaze into your ball?

RICKY: That's "balls" to you, dearie . . .

LENA: You mean?

RICKY: *(Nods.)* Uh huh . . . pluralssss . . .

LENA: More than one?

RICKY: See, Lena . . . there's hope for you, yet.

LENA: I love the word "yet."

RICKY: How 'bout we both say it out loud together?

LENA: What?

RICKY: Yet . . .

LENA: The word "yet?"

RICKY: Yep . . .

LENA: I know! Let's spell it . . .

RICKY: Out loud together?

LENA *nods.*

RICKY: Okay . . .

LENA *and* RICKY *move in face to face and hold hands on the table.*

RICKY: Ready?

LENA *nods.*

LENA *and* RICKY: *(Spell.)* Y . . . E . . . T . . .

They break apart in a fit of laughter.

RICKY: Whatever happened to "being a pet?"

LENA: And my dog. . . . Where's my dog? You promised me a dog. . . .

RICKY: How's the band?

LENA: Things are going good, thanks. . . . We're playing The Tom-Tom in two weeks.

RICKY: What night?

LENA: Wednesday.

RICKY: That's me and Antoine's first anniversary . . .

LENA: How sweet . . .

RICKY: He's planning a gastronomical, uh . . . fête . . . he calls it . . . with a tropical motif . . .

LENA: I'm doing a solo performance at Cat O'Nine Tails this weekend.

RICKY: Oh yeah? That's where we first met!

LENA: That's right! I'd forgotten.

RICKY: Uh—six months ago. You know, Lena . . . you said something, a second ago . . . about, how an image comes out of the blue. . . . I lived in this house when I was a kid. . . . Out back was a dog house, but we didn't have a dog . . . had to be summer . . . I wasn't in school. So, during the day . . . I'd squeeze through the hole . . . and curl up for hours, just dreaming inside. . . . *(Pause.)* You know . . . I'd like to go back and find that house . . .

LENA: Hey, Ricky. (RICKY *looks.*) I think you just did . . .

Pause. Music fades up.

RICKY: How's Meredith doing?

LENA: Same old. . . . Treats me like a king. *(RICKY laughs.)* She just
signed a new band . . . they're pretty good. . . .

RICKY: Yeah . . . Antoine . . . he's so fucking perfect. . . . *(Light begins
to fade.)* I keep asking myself, "What's wrong with this picture?"
. . . Nothing's missing, Lena. . . . *(Light out. Music starts fading.)*
I mean . . . why pick a card when nothing's missing? . . .

SCENE ONE:
ANTOINE & RICKY; *bedroom;*
late same afternoon

SYNTHESIS:
Bar walls swing back; music fades out; ANTOINE's *on the phone; joined in
mid-conversation; bedroom light rises when* ANTOINE *starts speaking.*

ANTOINE: *(Dressed formally, with phone in hand.)* No, not yet . . . Are
you crazy? *(Lights fade up.)* Contacting Kenny. . . . My ice sculpting
. . . I would just die, do you hear . . . I'd die on the spot, if . . . oh
. . . I can't even say it *(Winces.)* . . . Melted . . . there, okay . . . I'm
over it now. . . . No. . . . Play it safe. . . . Wait twenty minutes, no—
. . . wait half an hour . . . then have them wheel it out of the
freezer . . . you remember where it goes. . . . What do you mean
"what is it?" . . . Hmmph . . . I know who didn't take his smart
drugs today. . . . Well, Ken, it's a ship. . . . No, it's not the *HMS
Pinafore,* they did *Pirates* last season. . . . No, I don't know the
name of the ship. . . . It's Wagner. . . . Well, the San Francisco
Opera isn't paying me to listen to your problems. . . . Please . . .
uh huh, wait thirty minutes . . . now, be a doll and give the phone
to Meliberto. . . . Oh, really? . . . and you think he might've gone
back into the kitchen . . . Well, Ken, if I were you . . . and the boss
asked me to find someone . . . I truly believe, the first thing I'd do
. . . would be to call out the name of that someone. . . . That's it,
hon. . . . Good. . . . Scream it out loud. . . . Can you do it in G? . . .
Never mind. . . . What? . . . Who cares if they're all staring at you?
. . . Jesus Christ, Kenny! . . . Of course it's important . . . he's my
lucky charm. . . . Ha ha, very funny . . . don't you dare hang up
this phone. . . . Now, go. . . . Hurry . . . and Ken, don't forget . . .
cut the stems way back . . . thank you, I agree. . . . They just seem
so right for the garland. . . . Okay, toodaloo . . . put the phone

down, love. . . . *(ANTOINE sets phone on bed.)* So far so good . . .
doesn't sound too drunk . . . Come on, little feet . . . let's do shoes
and socks . . . *(Pause.)* Socks in the bathroom. . . . *(He stands.)* Oh,
Ricky . . . where art thou? . . . *(Exiting, ANTOINE turns SR, humming
"Goody Goody," then races back and sticks ear up to phone. Back to closet.
Gets shoes. Sits on bed. Phone ear to shoulder. ANTOINE puts on his socks
and shoes.)* Meliberto? . . . Como esta? . . . Y tu? . . . Y tu, Bueno. . . .
Y Kenny? Quanto? . . . Good. Tu? . . . Si . . . No . . . Si, right . . .
poquito muy bueno . . . as long as you're drinking with him. Que?
. . . No . . . just let the bisque simmer . . . ey . . . Cómo, Meliberto,
por favor, mi amigo . . . Cómo se dice, "Did you find the arugula?"
in Español? . . . Good . . . Where? . . . In with the cilantro . . . God,
now it's tainted! . . . I feel like a camel. . . . Qué? . . . A camel . . .
you know, like the straw that broke . . . it's nothing. . . . Look,
forget it. . . . Oh, see, ha ha. . . . You do comprende. . . . Sí . . .
Cancun forever! . . . Put Kenny back on. . . . I'm coming, hasta
pronto. . . . Adios, Amigo. . . . Is that you, Ricky?

RICKY: *(Offstage.)* Yeah . . .

ANTOINE: Hope you didn't eat . . . Kenny slow down . . . you're
slurring your words. . . .

RICKY: *(Entering.)* Do I have time to take a shower?

ANTOINE: *(Nods his head, pointing at the phone.)* Yes . . . yes, tell him to
stir it. . . . *(To RICKY)* Suit's in the closet, fresh from the cleaners . . .

RICKY: *(Opening the closet.)* Thanks . . . *(Looks for a tie.)*

ANTOINE: *(To phone.)* No . . . *(To RICKY.)* Ken . . . *(To phone.)* I was
talking to Ricky . . . uh huh, he just got home. . . . No, getting
undressed. . . . Stop . . . *(To RICKY.)* He's teasing us . . . *(To phone.)*
You homophobic brute . . . kiss, kiss, ciao. . . . We'll be there
before you know it. . . .

RICKY: *(Holding ties.)* Which one?

ANTOINE: Hello there . . .

RICKY: Red?

ANTOINE: *(Shakes head.* RICKY *puts back ties.)* Help. . . .

RICKY: What's wrong?

ANTOINE: Oh, nothing . . .

RICKY: *(Exiting.)* You need to use the bathroom?

ANTOINE: No . . . kiss . . . No hug . . . not even hello? . . .

RICKY: *(Enters and hugs* ANTOINE.*)* Hello . . . I'm sorry. . . .

ANTOINE: I accept. . . . Did you miss me?

RICKY: Sure did, Antoine. . . . All day long. . . .

ANTOINE: How sweet. . . . *(Breaks.)* And just where have you been . . . all day long?

RICKY: Oh, that's right. . . .

ANTOINE: Let me smell you.

RICKY: I forgot . . .

ANTOINE: What? His name?

RICKY: Who? . . . I ran into Lena

ANTOINE: You mean, Lena, "My Lena?"

RICKY: Yeah . . .

ANTOINE: Where? . . . At some bar?

ANTOINE *picks up phone.*

RICKY: Hey . . . I only had . . . one Calistoga. . . . *(*ANTOINE *dials.)* Who you calling?

ANTOINE: Go in the kitchen. . . .

RICKY: Why?

ANTOINE: Love . . .

RICKY: Should I bring back the I Can't Believe It's Not Butter?

ANTOINE: No, silly-willy. . . . Look on the counter. . . .

RICKY: You devil. . . . Did you buy me an orchid?

ANTOINE: No, a new creation . . . it's chestnut chutney. . . .

RICKY: Chutney?

ANTOINE: *(To phone.)* Meredith, How are you, dear? . . . Fine . . . it's me, Antoine. . . .

RICKY: What are you doing?

ANTOINE: *(To* RICKY.*)* Shhh . . . checking your story . . .

RICKY: Christ Almighty!

ANTOINE: *(To phone.)* Is Lena home, by any chance? May I speak with her please? . . . Thank you. . . . Cha-Cha-Cha . . . *(To* RICKY.*)* Not that I don't trust you . . . *(To phone.)* Hello, Lena, hello! . . . How's the baby she-talent? . . . Yessiree, big party tonight . . . I heard you ran into Ricky. . . . Yes, he certainly is, and what time did he leave? . . . Good. . . . and Meredith? . . . Good. . . . No, I didn't get a chance to talk with her. . . . Soon . . . let's . . . yes, I promise. . . . Sounds like fun, well, we're off to the opera. . . . You too. . . . (ANTOINE *hangs up.*)

RICKY: Has the jury reached a verdict?

ANTOINE: *(On knees.)* Oh, God, Ricky, how I need you tonight. . . .

RICKY: Not if I don't take a shower.

ANTOINE: *(Rising like a sprite.)* Wait, love . . . try the beige . . . *(Exiting to bathroom.)* I'll be out in a jiff. . . .

Pause.

RICKY: I don't know why you're so jealous of me.

ANTOINE: *(Offstage.)* Well, for one . . . you're ten years younger. . . .

RICKY: *(Holding beige tie.)* You really think the beige?

ANTOINE: *(Backing up into bedroom.)* Uh oh . . .

RICKY: What happened?

ANTOINE: It's . . . the toilet . . .

RICKY *stands behind* ANTOINE, *looking over* ANTOINE's *shoulder, into the bathroom.*

ANTOINE: The water's just swirling around . . .

RICKY: Well, water seeks it's own level . . .

ANTOINE: Don't make fun of me, Ricky.

RICKY: I'm not making fun of you. . . . *(Pause, both staring.)* Anyway, it doesn't look like it'll overflow . . .

ANTOINE *swirls into the room.* RICKY *enters the bathroom.*

ANTOINE: I don't have time for this. . . . It's a catastrophe, an omen . . . a dire portent . . .

RICKY: *(Entering.)* I'm gonna jump in the shower. . . .

ANTOINE: *(Runs past* RICKY.*)* Wait! *(Stops in doorway.)* The water stopped. . . .

RICKY: I turned off the valve.

ANTOINE: *(Hugs* RICKY.*)* Oh, lover . . . what would I do without you . . . ?

RICKY: *(Whispers.)* Drown?

ANTOINE: *(Breaks away.)* Did you taste the chutney?

RICKY: Sure did. . . . Yum-yum. (ANTOINE *eyes* RICKY *suspiciously.*) Exquisite flavors envelop my tongue. . . .

ANTOINE: Liar! *(Exits to kitchen.* RICKY *hangs up clothes.)* Mmmm, it's delicious. . . .

RICKY: Antoine . . . you could scrape off a railroad track and make it delicious. . . .

ANTOINE: Thanks. . . . *(Enters chewing.)* You really should try some. . . .

RICKY: I'm saving myself. . . .

ANTOINE: For whom?

RICKY: My appetite . . . *(Exits to bathroom.)* For your opera extravaganza . . .

ANTOINE: *(To closet.)* I don't know about the beige. . . . Maybe . . .

RICKY: *(Offstage.)* Uh oh . . .

ANTOINE: *(Jumps into bathroom.)* What now?

RICKY: The shower . . . *(Enters with* ANTOINE *on his tail.)* It's backing up sludge. . . .

ANTOINE: Sludge! *(Exits.)* I can't deal with this. . . .

RICKY: Better call a plumber. . . .

ANTOINE: *(Entering.)* Plumber? What plumber? I don't know any plumbers. . . .

RICKY *puts on* ANTOINE's *Cinderella coat.*

ANTOINE: What should I do? It's late! I forget— . . . do I own this apartment?

RICKY: *(Laughing.)* Maybe I'll wear this. . . .

ANTOINE: *(Laughs, charging* RICKY.*)* You put that back. . . .

RICKY: *(Dodging* ANTOINE.*)* What do you think?

ANTOINE: Put back my Cinderella coat . . . *(*ANTOINE *stops moving.)* Someday . . . she'll come along . . . and I'll fall desperately in love with her. . . .

RICKY: *(Removing coat.)* The first woman it fits, huh?

ANTOINE: *(Grabs coat from* RICKY *and hangs it up.)* It's too small for Lena. . . .

RICKY: I guess I'll do without the shower. . . .

ANTOINE: *(Removes* RICKY's *flight attendant jacket and puts it on.)* How about you . . . you big flirt . . . *(Pretends to serve a passenger.)* Forget the coffee or tea, hon. . . . *(Vamping around the room.)* Meet me in the lavatory. . . . The one on the right. . . . Hurry, while it's vacant. . . .

RICKY: Boy, are you warped. . . .

ANTOINE *hangs up* RICKY's *jacket and exits to bathroom.*

RICKY: You really think I'd do that?

ANTOINE: *(Passing by door to kitchen.)* It stopped. . . .

RICKY *stands motionless, staring at doorway.*

ANTOINE: *(Peeking back in door.)* Come on, hon . . . ¡Ándale! ¡Ándale! *(Exits.)* The opera waits for no one. . . .

Lights begin to fade.

ANTOINE: *(Offstage.)* Everything's fine. . . . Nothing's wrong. . . .

Pause.

RICKY: *(Quietly.)* Yet . . .

Lights fade.

SCENE TWO:
MEREDITH & LENA; *living room;*
late same afternoon

SYNTHESIS:
MEREDITH, *in place, begins lunging.* RICKY *exits.*
Living room lights rise slowly
on MEREDITH *doing her lunging exercise.*
Lunging is a cross between tai chi and step aerobics.

MEREDITH: *(Three lunges out facing* SL, *three* SR, *three* SL, LENA *enters and stands watching, three* SR, *turns* SL.) Oh, Lena . . . you startled me . . .

LENA: How's the lunging?

MEREDITH: Actually, you didn't startle me . . . I don't know why I said that . . . I just . . . didn't hear the door. . . . Fine, great . . .

LENA: You really think it helps?

MEREDITH: Who knows . . . *(Sitting.)* Believe me, I tried all that other shit. . . . Zen, motorcycles. *(Pause.)* How'd rehearsal go?

LENA: I'm charged!

MEREDITH: Good! *(Beckons.)* Come over here . . . sit down . . . *(Lena hesitates.)* Take a load off. . . .

LENA: *(Moving toward* MEREDITH.) Tambourine blew her amp. . . .

LENA *sits on the floor and leans back her head against* MEREDITH.

MEREDITH: *(Rubbing* LENA's *head.)* Well, some people need more attention than others . . .

LENA: I swear she did it on purpose. . . . You know, like . . . she had it up too high. . . .

MEREDITH: Out there, with people . . . shit happens.

Pause.

LENA: "Role Model" sounded really hot. . . .

MEREDITH: That song's gonna make you a star. . . .

LENA: You think so?

MEREDITH: I know so. . . .

LENA: Really?

MEREDITH: Uh huh . . . is that what you want?

LENA: Uh huh.

MEREDITH: Sing it for me.

LENA: What?

MEREDITH: Just the chorus.

LENA: I can't. . . .

MEREDITH: Come on. . . .

LENA: No.

MEREDITH: Why not?

LENA: Okay . . . *(Sits upright.)* We left . . . our babies . . . in the snowmobile . . . We hope . . . they'll be . . . alright. . . . We left . . . your dinner . . . in the microwave . . . just heat . . . it up . . . tonight. . . . *(Starts laughing.)* No more, I can't. . . .

MEREDITH: *(Laughing.)* It's a great song. . . . Ladies and Germs, and I do mean germs. . . . These are The Objects. . . .

LENA: I love that intro . . . I want to use it. . . .

MEREDITH: I thought it up for you today.

LENA: *(Somewhat disappointed.)* Oh . . .

MEREDITH: Is there something wrong with that?

LENA: No. . . . Yes, I mean, uh, no. . . .

MEREDITH: Well? . . . Which one?

LENA: I mean . . . just don't . . . let me forget it. . . .

MEREDITH: What?

LENA: That you thought it up for me. . . . Don't let me forget.

MEREDITH: You mean . . . you feel . . . you take me for granted?

LENA: *(Rises—crossing to window.)* I don't know, Merry . . . I guess so,

MEREDITH: You're my baby and I love you. . . . Don't forget that. . . .

LENA: *(Staring out the window.)* Did you ever have a dog?

Pause.

LENA: Did you ever have a dog?

MEREDITH: *(Turning.)* Is that a new piece?

LENA: No. I'm asking you a question.

MEREDITH: Oh . . . sorry . . . Did I ever have a dog? *(Rising.)* Yes . . . once . . . bit off my thumb. . . .

LENA: Huh?

MEREDITH: When I was eight. . . . Helluva story. . . .

Pause.

LENA: I'm gonna make it.

Pause.

LENA: I just wish I knew what "it" I'm gonna make. . . .

LENA *looks at* MEREDITH *and they laugh.*

MEREDITH: Guess who I ran into, today?

LENA: Who?

LENA *sits on divan.*

MEREDITH: *(Laughing.)* Claudia.

LENA: No!

MEREDITH: Yes . . .

LENA: Not "The" Ms. Sappho?

MEREDITH: They've got a new release. . . .

LENA: Where'd you see her?

MEREDITH: Outside The Keyhole . . . smoking a beedie. . . . Shit, I've gotta get a hold of Gentleman Ben. . . . *(Dials cell phone. Chuckles.)* That Claudia. . . . Hello, is this Ben? . . . No? Okay, I give . . . can I speak to him? . . . My, we're full of "no"s today. . . . He's not there? . . . His brother? Which one? . . . Tommy. . . . That's me, yes. . . . The dyke with dark hair. . . . What drug are you on, Tommy? What? In detox? Shit! He's got a gig tonight. . . . Where? . . . St. Agatha's . . . do you have the number? Never mind . . . (MEREDITH *ends call.*) Shit! Goddamn Ben's in detox (MEREDITH *keys 411.*) Son of a bitch missed three dates in July . . . *(To phone.)* Yes, San Francisco . . . St. Agatha's . . . which number? (LENA *rises.*) How about general information? . . . *(To* LENA.*)* You coming with me tonight?

LENA: No . . . I think I'll work on my piece . . . it needs it. . . .

MEREDITH: *(Dialing.)* Okay . . . *(To phone.)* Yes, I'd like to speak with a patient. . . . (LENA *exits.*) Uh, Benjamin, what's his last name? I'll have to dig out the contract . . . Gentleman Ben. . . . He's a musician . . . he's in detox. . . . Yes, I'll hold. . . . *(Looks around for* LENA.*)* Radiology? I don't need radiology . . . I'm looking for Gentleman Ben. . . . Well, let me speak to your boss's boss. . . . *(Looks out the window. Pause. Lights begin to fade. Turns* SL.*)* No . . . I never had a dog . . .

Lights out. Techno beat rises.

FLASHBACK:
LENA, MEREDITH, ANTOINE & RICKY;
dressing room at the Cat O' Nine Tales; six months earlier

SYNTHESIS:
Mirror opens out CS. LENA *sits in front of mirror. Techno beat fades.*

LENA: *(Rehearsing act in mirror.)* There are two kinds of people on the planet . . . schizophrenic. You are either one or the other. I personally have been diagnosed as having nine distinct personalities. My doctor calls me the ultimate team player. . . .

MEREDITH: *(Entering dressing room.)* Claudia's about halfway done. How you feeling?

LENA: Good and plenty loose. How's she doing?

MEREDITH: A little subdued. The crowd needs you.

ANTOINE: *(Entering dressing room trailed by* RICKY.*)* Hello, Lena, Hello!

MEREDITH: *(Displeased.)* Look who's here—

LENA: *(Lights up.)* Antoine!

ANTOINE: See? I told you I would come. *(Points.)* This is Ricky.

MEREDITH *snarls.*

ANTOINE: Are we interrupting?

LENA: Not at all.

ANTOINE: *(Points.)* That's Lena.

RICKY: Hello, Lena.

LENA: Hi.

MEREDITH: Most people drop in after the show.

LENA: That's Meredith.

ANTOINE: *(To* MEREDITH.*)* I knew Lena before you did.

MEREDITH: *(To* ANTOINE.) So, did you two meet online?

LENA: Be nice. It's true—you know. I took his cooking class. What was it? Two years ago or—

ANTOINE: *(Phone rings.)* What is it, Ken? . . . What? Hold on! *(Leaving dressing room for hall* USR.*)* What do you mean the gruyere turned black? That's impossible. . . .

MEREDITH: *(Phone rings.)* Hello. . . . Yes, Ben. It's me. *(Leaving dressing room for hall* DSL.*)* No, I never loan clients money, Ben.

ANTOINE's *&* MEREDITH's *conversations overlaps as they do.*

ANTOINE: The squid ink? Are you kidding me? How could this happen? Tell me the reason I cannot leave you alone in the restaurant for ten minutes— *(Listens.)*

MEREDITH: You should be at the gig now, Ben. You are. Well, that's a plus. Just put the drinks on the tab like you always do. . . . Then why do you need money? *(Listens.)*

In the silence, RICKY *stares at* LENA *looking in mirror. Long pause.*

RICKY: I look forward to seeing your show. . . .

LENA: *(Looks at* RICKY *in mirror.)* That's nice. . . .

Lights fade. Techno beat rises.

SEGUE TWO:
LENA *&* RICKY; *bar;*
two weeks from Segue One

SYNTHESIS:
Techno beat rises. MEREDITH *exits. Bar walls swing open.*
Chairs and table in place. RICKY *sits* SR; LENA SL.

LENA: I don't know, it's like . . . I got to thinking . . . you know . . . about, what you said. . . . *(Bar light rises. Techno beat fades.)* So I called you . . .

RICKY: And here we are . . .

LENA: She's self-sufficient . . . she doesn't need me.

RICKY: I'm on the same plane as you . . .

LENA: At least you get to travel . . . I mean, Meredith. . . . we're always together. . . .

RICKY: I'm lucky. . . .

LENA: I'll say. . . .

RICKY: Thanks to Antoine, I only work twelve days every five weeks. . . . I'm counter-productive. . . .

LENA: I know how you feel. . . .

RICKY: He pays the rent. . . .

LENA: Been anywhere interesting?

RICKY: Alaska . . . no biggie . . . the final frontier.

Pause.

RICKY: I'm glad you called.

LENA: I had to talk with somebody.

RICKY: Well . . . I guess I'll have to do.

LENA: Oh, Dick . . . you're sweet.

RICKY: Dick? No one calls me that . . . not since school. . . .

LENA: I like it . . . I mean, it seems to fit.

RICKY: I'm not touching that line. . . .

LENA: Huh? Oh. *(Laughs.)* Well, you just look like a Dick.

RICKY: That one, either. . . .

Pause.

LENA: I don't know what to do . . . I'm happy. . . .

Pause.

LENA: She's ten years older.

LENA *touches* RICKY's *foot under the table.*

RICKY: *(Uneasy. Looks under table.)* What?

LENA: How old are you?

RICKY: Thirty.

LENA: I'm twenty-five.

RICKY: *(Responding to* LENA's *foot.)* Yeah, Antoine's ten years older. . . .
Lena, look. . . .

LENA: At our feet?

RICKY: Don't tell Antoine.

LENA: Never . . .

RICKY: I was married.

LENA: You?

RICKY: When I was twenty-three . . . it didn't last. . . .

LENA: What was her name?

RICKY: Gretchen . . .

LENA: Gretchen . . . Gretchen . . . I don't know any Gretchens.

RICKY: I did. . . .

LENA: What happened?

RICKY: I quit school. . . .

LENA: High school?

RICKY: College. . . . We ran off to Europe.

LENA: Where?

RICKY: She left me in Belgium. . . .

LENA: Belgium?

RICKY: I think she had the marriage annulled. . . .

LENA: Poor boy . . .

Pause. Techno music rises.

RICKY: *(Sitting up.)* I'm very attracted to you right now, Lena.

LENA: Is that what's going on?

RICKY: I don't feel . . . like . . . a "gay" man. . . .

LENA: What does that— . . . I don't, either.

They hold hands and continue footsies. Techno beat rises.

RICKY: You should've seen him . . . Antoine . . . for our anniversary . . . the meal he cooked . . . roast pig. . . . We wound up doing the hula together. . . .

LENA: Merry . . . Meredith . . . I call her Merry . . . It's like . . . I can do no wrong. . . . *(Light begins to fade.)* She says I'm her gift. . . . She's so supportive. . . . Of me, my art . . . the band . . . everything. . . . *(Light fades.)* Like I said . . . I can do no wrong. . . .

Lights out.

SCENE THREE:
LENA, MEREDITH, ANTOINE & RICKY;
living room; one month later

SYNTHESIS:
Bar wall closes. LENA *sits on stage against divan. Techno beat fades.*

LENA: *(Rehearsing performance piece.)* Drive-thru. . . . No. . . . Fast-food. . . . Yeah . . . Fast-food Cruel-world Drive-thru Window. . . . Meet my servants . . . behind the counter . . . Pimple and Zit. . . . That's Zit on the right. . . . Leaving, yes . . . Pimple on the left. . . . I don't know which one I like better . . . they both asked me out. . . . Let me tell you, on other planets . . . it's no different. . . . Last month, no . . . July . . . in July . . . I was kidnapped by aliens . . . and I went to a fast-food . . . place . . . and the kid had little rust stains on his face . . . and guess what? He asked me out, too. . . . I didn't put out for him, though. . . . I think it was the metal condom that turned me off. . . . I wonder what they do with all the pickles they hold? . . . Where are they now? The one in the classy high-rent district has Shrimp McScampi, hon . . . Oh, I don't know if we can afford it . . . Global Village . . . Big Morocco, hold the mayo. . . . Now I will play each separate french fry in your bag. . . . I'm crispy. . . . I'm overcooked. . . . Don't you love me? . . .

MEREDITH *enters and takes off her shoes, listening to* LENA.

LENA: Excuse me, but . . . my fries need global warming. . . . I'm soggy. . . . I'm salty. . . . Don't you love me? . . . Will that be for here or to go?

MEREDITH *laughs.*

LENA: *(Looking up.)* You like the piece?

MEREDITH *nods.*

LENA: How goes the world?

MEREDITH: It's a jungle out there. . . . *(Fakes Tarzan yell.)*

LENA: That's it! . . . New attraction. . . . Barnyard Safari. . . . Chop your own beef. . . . Kill your own burger. . . .

MEREDITH: I better do some lunges. *(Takes position.)* Shake off reality. . . . *(Begins lunging.)*

LENA: No, Zit! . . . Stop, Pimple! . . . Here's your change, sir. . . . Want a free tattoo?

MEREDITH: *(Stops lunging.)* You know what I saw on Market today?

LENA *shakes her head.*

MEREDITH: A dead man . . . walking around. He was dead! Like this . . . *(Places hand under chin, closes eyes and walks.)* Just walking around. He was sleeping . . . or something. It's crazy! And he had a splint on his middle finger . . . *(Points.)* Here . . . made from a plastic knife. . . . You know the kind you see . . . at parties. . . . Looneytoons! . . . A dead man with a plastic knife on his finger. . . .

MEREDITH *starts lunging again. Lena rises and shuffles her feet.*

LENA: Um . . . Merry?

MEREDITH: *(In mid-lunge.)* What?

LENA: Uh . . . I don't know how to say this. . . .

MEREDITH: *(Stops lunging.)* Say what? . . .

LENA *turns away from* MEREDITH.

MEREDITH: What? . . . Just say it. . . .

LENA: *(Turns back around.)* I'm moving out.

Pause.

MEREDITH: Is it the lunging?

LENA: No . . .

MEREDITH: Is it Tambourine?

LENA: What? . . . Are you kidding?

MEREDITH: I just figure it's Tambourine, you know . . . You're always complaining about her. . . . That's what people do . . . they use anger to hide their true feelings. . . .

LENA: I'm moving in with Ricky.

MEREDITH: Is she the one that carried your cymbals at The Argyle? The blonde with the cute little butt?

LENA: No . . . *(Thinks twice, excited.)* No . . . *(Pause.)* Antoine's Ricky.

MEREDITH: A man? . . . You're leaving me for "A Man?"

LENA: I don't know how it happened, Merry.

MEREDITH: I can't believe it!

LENA: Don't be mad. . . .

MEREDITH: What? His dick bigger than the one I bought you? . . . *(Climbing out the window.)* A man . . . God, how humiliating. . . .

LENA: *(Sticking head out the window.)* What are you doing?

MEREDITH: Don't worry, Lena . . . I'm not gonna jump. . . .

LENA *paces the room all flustered.*

MEREDITH: *(Calmly.)* What a nice day. . . . Not a cloud in the sky.

LENA: *(Stops pacing.)* Is the fog coming in?

MEREDITH *doesn't answer.*

LENA: *(Starts pacing again.)* Look, Merry . . . I talked to Ricky. . . . He and Antoine are coming over.

MEREDITH: Goody . . . a showdown.

LENA: They'll be here any second.

MEREDITH: I know . . . I can see them.

LENA: *(Returning to window.)* Where?

MEREDITH: There . . . on the street.

LENA: *(Looking down.)* Oh . . .

MEREDITH: Hello, slimy turds!

LENA: Be nice. . . .

MEREDITH: They can't hear me. . . .

Buzzer rings.

LENA: *(Back in.)* I'd better buzz them in.

Lena exits. Pause.

MEREDITH: *(Sings the Beatles' "She's Leaving Home.")* Wednesday morning at five o'clock . . . as the day begins . . . silently closing the bedroom door . . . leaving the note that she hoped would say more . . . she goes downstairs to the kitchen, clutching her handkerchief. . . .

ANTOINE: *(Offstage.)* Lena, Lena, you look fabulous, darling.

LENA: *(Offstage.)* Thanks . . .

ANTOINE: *(Offstage.)* Close the door, Ricky.

RICKY *groans.*

ANTOINE: *(Entering.)* Lovely, lovely . . . *(Spins.)* Meredith has such good taste.

LENA *and* RICKY *enter.* RICKY *wears a plastic jacket with a map of the world on it.*

ANTOINE: *(To* LENA.*)* Where is she?

LENA: *(Points.)* Out on the ledge. . . . *(Whispers to* RICKY.*)* I can't believe you didn't tell him.

RICKY *shrugs.*

ANTOINE: *(Reacting as if nothing were wrong, sticks head out the window.)* Hi, Big Girl. . . . What you doing?

MEREDITH: Enjoying the view. . . .

RICKY: *(Whispering.)* I couldn't do it. . . .

ANTOINE: Can you see Mount Davidson?

MEREDITH: She's leaving home. . . .

ANTOINE: Who? . . . Lena?

ANTOINE *turns to* LENA. LENA *nods.* RICKY *stiffens up.* LENA *turns to* RICKY. RICKY *steps back.* ANTOINE *realizes the "who" is* RICKY.

ANTOINE: Oh, God . . . Ricky, how could you? . . . My Lena? . . . No . . . *(Climbs out onto the ledge.)* No . . .

RICKY: Antoine, be careful!

LENA: *(Grabbing* RICKY.*)* Where'd you get this jacket . . . it's god-awful . . .

RICKY: What do you mean? . . . I love this jacket. . . .

ANTOINE: *(On ledge, to* MEREDITH.*)* Are you going to jump?

MEREDITH: No . . .

ANTOINE: Why not?

MEREDITH: It could be worse down there. . . .

LENA: What's it made out of . . . plastic?

RICKY: Hey . . . with this jacket . . . people talk to me, wherever I go. . . . You look great.

LENA *leads* RICKY *offstage to the kitchen, where they start petting.*

MEREDITH: I might come back as a tree, or worse . . . a "man." . . .

ANTOINE: What's wrong with being a man?

MEREDITH: Please!

ANTOINE: They pay attention to you. . . .

MEREDITH: Worthless . . .

ANTOINE: More than women. . . . Is that a fire over there?

MEREDITH: You little twit. . . . If you would've spent more time keeping your man happy instead of cooking . . . soufflés . . . and chopping . . . mushrooms . . . I'd still have Lena. . . .

ANTOINE: Hmmph . . . Well, I'm not the one who galavants around night and day. . . . You know, sweet-talking people. . . . Sign here, hon. . . . Love your hair . . . and all that . . .

MEREDITH: Watch it!

RICKY: *(Offstage.)* You smell great. . . .

LENA: *(Offstage.)* Kiss me again . . .

ANTOINE: *(Peeks in window.)* Oh, God . . . I think they're smooching in there. . . . *(Back on ledge.)* I can hear them—whoahhh!

ANTOINE *almost falls off the ledge.* MEREDITH *catches him.*

MEREDITH: Look out, you fool . . .

ANTOINE: Oh, Meredith, wow! You saved my life. . . .

MEREDITH: Big deal. . . .

LENA: *(Offstage.)* We better go check on them. . . .

RICKY: *(Offstage.)* See how they're doing. . . .

ANTOINE: Well, it's a big deal to me. . . .

LENA *and* RICKY *enter.*

MEREDITH: I should've let you drop. . . .

ANTOINE: I've never been in an ambulance before. . . .

LENA: *(Sticks head out the window.)* Come in, both of you. . . . Down off the ledge. . . . Come on . . . *(Helps* ANTOINE *back in.)* Come on, Meredith. . . .

ANTOINE: *(To* RICKY.*)* I almost fell . . . *(Pointing.)* She saved my life. . . .

MEREDITH: *(Climbing in. To* LENA.*)* So . . . now it's Meredith. . . .

ANTOINE: *(Turns away from* RICKY.*)* Traitor!

Pause. ANTOINE *and* MEREDITH *stand face to face pouting with their arms folded.*

LENA: Come on, you guys . . . it's not so bad. . . .

RICKY: Look . . . I'm not very good at being noble. . . .

MEREDITH: Shut up, you little twerp. . . .

ANTOINE: Don't talk to him that way.

LENA: Come on, Merry. . . .

MEREDITH: Now it's Merry. . . .

ANTOINE: I'm happy for you, Lena. . . . *(Drops, grabbing* RICKY *by the knees.)* Don't leave me, Ricky.

RICKY *and* LENA *exchange glances, then skylight (look up).*

MEREDITH: Know of anyone that needs a room?

ANTOINE: *(Rises. To* LENA.*)* You have your own room?

MEREDITH: Butt out, Antoine.

ANTOINE: No wonder . . .

MEREDITH: You heard me. . . . Go cook some pasta. . . .

LENA: You two stop fighting. . . .

RICKY: I don't know what to say. . . .

MEREDITH: How 'bout, "See you later . . . "

RICKY: We're getting a place together . . . me and Lena. . . .

MEREDITH: Glad you got that out of your system. . . .

ANTOINE: *(To* LENA.*)* Have you looked around? . . . *(Out.)* Rent's are sky-high. . . .

LENA: We'll find something . . . I . . . I love Dick. . . .

ANTOINE: I know what you mean, honey. . . .

MEREDITH: *(Over* ANTOINE*; to* RICKY*)* Where'd you get the jacket?

ANTOINE: It's his conversation piece. . . .

MEREDITH: *(Crossing, points nonchalantly.)* I've been there. . . .

RICKY: Where?

MEREDITH: Nepal . . . the Himalayas . . .

RICKY: Really?

MEREDITH: Trekking . . .

ANTOINE: I stayed on a houseboat . . . once, in Kashmir . . . for three days with Daniel . . . *(Lights begin to fade.* LENA *turns her back, feeling left out.)* It was splendid . . .

MEREDITH: I've been . . . *(Points.)* there . . . and there. . . .

ANTOINE: Have you ever been to Egypt?

MEREDITH: *(Turning to* ANTOINE.*)* No . . . how is it?

ANTOINE: Hot . . .

MEREDITH: Hot?

RICKY *grabs* LENA. *Lights fade.*

RICKY: Very hot . . .

Techno beat rises. Light out. LENA *&* MEREDITH *off.* ANTOINE *&* RICKY *in place.*

SCENE FOUR:
RICKY *and* ANTOINE;
bedroom; two weeks later

SYNTHESIS:
ANTOINE *in closet.* RICKY *on phone. Lights rise as* RICKY *starts speaking.*

RICKY: *(On phone.)* Yes, who is this? . . . Damien? . . . Damien, this is Richard Best . . . I need my flight schedule for next week, yeah . . . The twenty-third. . . . Thanks, Damien. . . . What? The pilot drove through a rental car lot . . . They were filming a commercial. . . . Far out. . . . Okay. . . . *(On hold, aside.)* Where the hell is Antoine? I know he's here, I saw his car. . . . *(To phone.)* Yes, Damien . . . when? . . . Friday, Flight 66 . . . Departing SFO 4:15 p.m. . . . Okay, great . . . Yeah, thanks again. . . . *(Hangs up.)* I know you're here, Antoine. . . .

RICKY *starts to leave the bedroom.* ANTOINE *sighs from inside the closet.* RICKY *stops and stares at the closet.*

RICKY: Are you in the closet?

Pause.

RICKY: What are you doing?

ANTOINE: Does it matter?

RICKY *opens the closet doors.*

ANTOINE: *(Stationary.)* Remember when . . . I bought you . . . that shirt?

RICKY: Christ Almighty . . .

ANTOINE: The white one?

RICKY: You think this is easy?

ANTOINE: You're leaving me, aren't you?

RICKY: I fell in love . . . the same way I fell in love with you. . . .

ANTOINE: You picked her up in an airport bar?

RICKY: Not the same way, but . . . I fell in love. . . . *(Kneels.)* Don't get me wrong . . . the past year with you was the best of my life. . . .

ANTOINE: Thirteen months . . .

RICKY: You gave so much. . . .

ANTOINE: He speaks past tense. . . .

RICKY: You're incredible, Antoine. . . . Your needs don't take . . .

ANTOINE: And I cook a mean grapefruit curry. . . .

RICKY: And you cook a mean grapefruit curry. . . .

Pause. RICKY *unbuttons his shirt, takes it off and hangs it up.*

RICKY: You want me to put on the shirt?

ANTOINE *shakes his head.*

RICKY: Will that make you happy?

ANTOINE *shakes his head harder.*

RICKY: Please, Antoine, for God's sake, please, come out of the closet . . .

ANTOINE: I did that already . . . years ago.

RICKY: I can't believe . . . I'm playing a straight man.

RICKY *shuts the closet doors and begins to take off his pants.* ANTOINE *pushes open* SR *closet door and stares at* RICKY.

RICKY: *(Struggling with pants, one leg off, lets go.)* Wanna have sex, one last time? . . . Is that it?

ANTOINE: *(Climbing out of closet.)* What do you know about women?

RICKY: For Christ's sake . . .

ANTOINE: A young woman?

RICKY: What do I know about men, for that matter?

ANTOINE: Well . . . you are one. . . .

RICKY: Yes . . . I am that. . . .

ANTOINE: You think you're the only one in love with her?

RICKY: Who? Lena? . . . I thought the coat didn't fit. . . .

ANTOINE: I adore women. . . .

RICKY: It doesn't fit me, either.

ANTOINE: It was love at first sight.

RICKY: With Lena?

ANTOINE: Uh huh. . . . She came waltzing into my cooking class at the culinary academy. . . . She was only nineteen. . . .

RICKY: *(Excited.)* I wish I could've seen her then. . . .

ANTOINE: Stop it, you beast. . . .

RICKY: Sorry . . .

ANTOINE: You're breaking my heart. . . . *(Breaks back.)* We became friends . . . I was . . . her confidante. . . . She told me everything. . . .

RICKY: What did she tell you? . . . I want all the dirt. . . .

ANTOINE: Richard, please . . . I'm baring my soul. . . .

ANTOINE *holds dramatic pause.*

ANTOINE: She's no slut, if that's what you mean. . . .

RICKY: That's what I mean. . . .

ANTOINE: I was with Daniel then . . . madly in love. . . . Lena came along. . . . He was insanely jealous of her. . . . *(ANTOINE laughs wistfully.)* Funny, now you . . . you'll be with her. . . .

RICKY: *(Stares off.)* Yeah . . .

ANTOINE: I can't believe you'll be living so close to the restaurant. . . .

RICKY: We'll drop in for dinner. . . .

ANTOINE: I'm off Monday and Tuesday. . . .

RICKY: Remember the night Luis caught on fire? . . .

ANTOINE *nods.*

RICKY: He came running by me . . . his back in flames. . . .

ANTOINE: The mayor was in the room. . . .

RICKY: I was sitting at the bar. . . .

ANTOINE: I think he had Cioppino. . . .

RICKY: Lucky it was raining out. . . .

ANTOINE: You had just moved in . . . remember?

RICKY *nods.* ANTOINE *looks at his picture on the wall and then in the closet.*

RICKY: We had some good times together. . . .

ANTOINE *exits to kitchen.*

RICKY: *(Removing pants.)* What are you doing?

Pause.

ANTOINE *returns and looks in the drawer of nightstand.*

RICKY: What are you looking for?

ANTOINE: Thumbtacks . . .

RICKY: What for?

ANTOINE: I'm going to hang my picture in the closet to keep me
company. . . .

RICKY: Come on, Antoine. *(Pause.)* They're in the second drawer,
next to the sink. . . .

ANTOINE: *(Breaks down before leaving.)* Oh!

RICKY: What now?

ANTOINE: He knows where my thumbtacks are. . . .

Pause.

RICKY: Antoine . . . *(Antoine looks.)* I'll love you forever. . . .

ANTOINE *closes in and grabs* RICKY *by the crotch. They stare at one another.
The spark is gone.*

ANTOINE *lets go of* RICKY. *The buzzer rings.* ANTOINE *exits.* RICKY *stands
motionless.*

ANTOINE: *(Offstage.)* Who is it? . . . Taxi? . . . I didn't call a taxi. . . .
Do you have the right building? . . . Oh, that's Greg . . . downstairs
. . . hold on . . . (ANTOINE *yells out the window)* Greg! Greg! . . .
(Lights begin to fade.) Just wait, driver . . . he'll be down in a minute
. . . Greg! Greg! . . . Your taxi's waiting. . . . *(Lights fade out.)*

SEGUE THREE:
ANTOINE & MEREDITH;
bar; one month later

SYNTHESIS:
Techno beat rises. Bar walls swing open. Chairs and table in place.
ANTOINE *sits* SR; MEREDITH, SL. LENA & RICKY *wait backstage.*

ANTOINE: I bought them a gift, you know . . . cute little something . . . happy trails and all that . . .

Bar light rises.

MEREDITH: Matching towels, no doubt . . .

ANTOINE: Lena was home . . . looked great. . . . Oh, to be young . . .

MEREDITH: God forbid . . .

ANTOINE: Ricky was flying the friendly skies . . .

MEREDITH: I went sky diving last week . . . the chute opened . . .

ANTOINE: You really should stop by and say hello . . .

MEREDITH: Can the biofeedback.

ANTOINE: Meredith, Meredith, why so glum? . . . You should be happy for them . . .

MEREDITH: *Them* was a movie with giant ants. . . . Scared the shit out of me as a kid. . . .

ANTOINE: World got you down?

MEREDITH: How do you deal with giant ants?

ANTOINE: I don't know, I guess . . . just cover 'em with chocolate . . . and sell 'em by the side of the road. . . . (MEREDITH *laughs.*) Remember that awful craze? . . . Now, it's sun-dried tomatoes . . .

MEREDITH: Antoine, thanks. . . . You made me laugh. . . .

ANTOINE: Post-partum depression . . . think nothing of it. . . .

MEREDITH: You know, you're right. . . . What more do I want? . . .
Part of me's in her. . . . I should be happy. . . .

Pause.

MEREDITH: I am happy. . . . I mean, it's not like I'm out here cruising
the bars . . . in order to fill . . . a void, or something like that. . . .
It's more like, I'm out here . . . creating the void. . . . There is no
void. . . . It's scary. . . . So what, I'm a dyke . . . I prefer women . . .
they're easy on the eyes, they look good on your arm. *(Pause.)*
They don't make me chafe. . . . In that respect, I'm as straight as
the next fella. . . .

ANTOINE: How dare you accuse me of cruising the bars. . . .

MEREDITH *laughs.* ANTOINE *joins her.*

ANTOINE: Come to think of it, I did meet, Ricky in a bar . . . of all
places, an airport bar. . . . You know how they say, that you never
see anyone you meet at the airport again? Well, honey—we were
the exception. . . . There I was . . . fresh off the plane . . . home
from a week in Chicago. . . . *(Pause.)* I wanted a drink . . . ordered
a double . . . wound up in a bed at the Something Suites. . . .

MEREDITH: Yeah, I met Lena at a CD release for some crazy band
called Bozo the Noun . . .

ANTOINE: What a strange name.

MEREDITH: You're telling me. . . . They wrote all their lyrics, only
with nouns. . . . Lena sat in on drums . . . I sat in on her. . . .

ANTOINE: You know, I can't remember . . . the first thing Ricky said
. . . but the second was, "Hey . . . do you fool around?" . . . He
looked so cute, I just had to say, "I'm a sucker for a man who
wears blue." . . .

MEREDITH: It never goes away . . .

ANTOINE: Not on your life . . . *(Pause.)* Me, I'm still mourning
Daniel . . .

Pause. The moment swells for both with many possibilities. Their losses. Joy. They might be good together. In the end, they realize they have a new friend. Their ups find one another and MEREDITH *nearly breaks down.*

ANTOINE: You really should see her. . . .

MEREDITH: I know . . . I know. . . .

ANTOINE: Life's, as they say, what you make it, sans bullshit . . . *(Lights begin to fade.)* You know what I got them? A bread machine! Presto-Jiffy, fresh, warm bread. . . . Lena, her eyes . . . I think she just loved it. . . . *(Lights fade.)* I forgot to bring yeast, so we couldn't try it out. . . .

FINALE:
RICKY & LENA;
home; same time

SYNTHESIS:
Bar walls close. RICKY *and* LENA *in place, against* SR *and* SL *bar walls respectively. Techno beat fades. Low overhead lights rise softly.*

RICKY: There was a dog on the flight that nobody claimed.

LENA: That's so sad. . . . He or she?

RICKY: I don't know.

LENA: Think we can keep it?

RICKY: I'll call up the landlord.

LENA: Where is it now?

RICKY: In a cage at the airport.

LENA: We have to do something.

RICKY: The lease says, "No pets."

Lights begin to fade.

LENA: What should we call it?

RICKY: How 'bout, Creation?

LENA: That's nice.

Pause.

RICKY: I love you. . . .

Lights fade.

LENA: Hmmm . . .

THE END

SILENCE

Nat King Cole's "When I Fall in Love" fills up the air we breathe.

{Promise fulfilled.}

PETER CARLAFTES is a New York-based author, poet, playwright, and performer. His previous books include *A Year on Facebook* (humor), *Drunkyard Dog*, and *I Fold With the Hand I Was Dealt* (poetry), and *Triumph for Rent (Three Plays)*.

Carlaftes was co-artistic director of Marilyn Monroe Memorial Theater in San Francico from 1992 to 2000. He is currently co-director of Three Rooms Press. He lives in New York City.

Recent and Forthcoming Books from Three Rooms Press

FICTION

Meagan Brothers
Weird Girl and What's His Name

Ron Dakron
Hello Devilfish!

Michael T. Fournier
Hidden Wheel
Swing State

Janet Hamill
Tales from the Eternal Café
(Introduction by Patti Smith)

Eamon Loingsigh
Light of the Diddicoy

Aram Saroyan
Still Night in L.A.

Richard Vetere
The Writers Afterlife
Champagne and Cocaine

MEMOIR & BIOGRAPHY

Nassrine Azimi and
Michel Wasserman
Last Boat to Yokohama:
The Life and Legacy of
Beate Sirota Gordon

Richard Katrovas
Raising Girls in Bohemia:
Meditations of an American
Father; A Memoir in Essays

Judith Malina
Moon Poem

Stephen Spotte
My Watery Self:
Memoirs of a Marine Scientist

PHOTOGRAPHY-MEMOIR

Mike Watt
On & Off Bass

SHORT STORY ANTHOLOGY

Dark City Lights: New York Stories
edited by Lawrence Block

Have a NYC I, II & III:
New York Short Stories;
edited by Peter Carlaftes
& Kat Georges

HUMOR

Peter Carlaftes
A Year on Facebook

MIXED MEDIA

John S. Paul
Sign Language: A Painter's
Notebook (photography, poetry
and prose)

TRANSLATIONS

Thomas Bernhard
On Earth and in Hell
(selected poems of
Thomas Bernhard with English
translations by Peter Waugh)

Patrizia Gattaceca
Isula d'Anima / Soul Island
(poems by the author
in Corsican with English
translations)

César Vallejo | Gerard Malanga
Malanga Chasing Vallejo
(selected poems of César Vallejo
with English translations
and additional notes by
Gerard Malanga)

George Wallace
EOS: Abductor of Men
(selected poems of George
Wallace with Greek translations)

DADA

Maintenant: A Journal of
Contemporary Dada Writing & Art
(Annual, since 2008)

PLAYS

Madeline Artenberg &
Karen Hildebrand
The Old In-and-Out

Peter Carlaftes
Triumph For Rent (3 Plays)
Teatrophy (3 More Plays)

POETRY COLLECTIONS

Hala Alyan
Atrium

Peter Carlaftes
DrunkYard Dog
I Fold with the Hand I Was Dealt

Thomas Fucaloro
It Starts from the Belly and Blooms
Inheriting Craziness is Like
a Soft Halo of Light

Kat Georges
Our Lady of the Hunger

Robert Gibbons
Close to the Tree

Israel Horovitz
Heaven and Other Poems

David Lawton
Sharp Blue Stream

Jane LeCroy
Signature Play

Philip Meersman
This is Belgian Chocolate

Jane Ormerod
Recreational Vehicles on Fire
Welcome to the Museum of Cattle

Lisa Panepinto
On This Borrowed Bike

George Wallace
Poppin' Johnny

THREE ROOMS PRESS

Three Rooms Press | New York, NY | Current Catalog: www.threeroomspress.com
Three Rooms Press books are distributed by PGW/Perseus: www.pgw.com

CPSIA information can be obtained at www.ICGtesting.com
Printed in the USA
LVOW07s0959050215

425825LV00002B/10/P

9 781941 110133